HOME IS WHERE THE HURT IS

HOME
is where the
HURT IS

Guidance for all victims of
sexual abuse in the home and for those
who support them

JANINE TURNER

THORSONS PUBLISHING GROUP

First published 1989

© Janine Turner, 1989

British Library Cataloguing in Publication Data

Turner, Janine, 1953-
   Home is where the hurt is: surviving
   sexual abuse.
   1. Sexual abuse victims
   I. Title
   362.8'8

ISBN 0 7225 1631 2

Published by Thorsons Publishers Limited, Wellingborough, Northamptonshire NN8 2RQ, England

Typeset by MJL Limited, Hitchin, Hertfordshire

Printed and bound in Great Britain by Woolnough Bookbinding Limited, Irthlingborough, Northamptonshire

10 9 8 7 6 5 4 3 2

This book is dedicated to John — an excellent psychologist; a patient teacher; an understanding friend who taught me how to survive.

'All things are possible'.

Contents

Acknowledgements

This book is not one voice, but many, and I would like to thank those who have so willingly shared their experiences. For them it was not easy. They still live with the fear of what people will think about the things that have happened to them in their lives. Their names have been changed, but their words are their own. I hope that through their sharing, there will be an opportunity for others to perhaps experience in some small way some of their pain and sadness, realizing what it is like to live in the aftermath of sexual abuse. We have a right to be heard, and we are not alone. There are many thousands more who suffer today in silence.

Thank you, John and Eddy, for your time and your patience. You have become a part of my own recovery.

My thanks goes also to Hilary Eldridge for sharing her work with sex offenders, and to those men who so willingly shared their feelings so that we might better understand the problems of sexual abuse as a whole. I believe it is important to hear both sides of the experience and to keep an open mind.

Different things work for different people, and contributions made by the various agencies concerned are invaluable. Thank you. Hopefully, by offering an insight into the way in which they work, we will in the future take away some of the stigma for sufferers reaching out for help.

I am also grateful to my family, to husband Mike, and to Joanne, who both offered such understanding and support during the preparation of this book.

And perhaps most important of all, I would like to thank my publishers, who believed in my work enough to offer me this voice.

Introduction

I do not profess to be an expert on sexual abuse. I am an explorer, a graduate of experience. I have learned from my own journey through life. I know what it feels like to sexually abused, and can therefore understand the needs of survivors and know how much our past influences our present.

There are many who have shared their experiences within this book, and I am proud to be able to offer them a voice. If, in sharing something of what we have learned, we can help another come to terms and accept their experiences enough to be able to live better with the kind of person they are today, then for us, the reliving of these experiences has been worthwhile. We cannot ignore our past; it happened. It remains a part of us today, and we can use it to help others who may feel isolated, desperate and alone. We believe in making past experience work *for* us instead of *against* us, making good come out of all that bad. Books cannot teach us about life, but experience can. Experience is the greatest teacher of them all.

In my first book, *A Crying Game* (Mainstream, 1984), I share my experience of living as a battered woman. While writing it, I realized that there was much more that I could not remember. Just as a car's headlights search in the dark, the book highlighted those images from my past which I see today. The blanks in between I knew would come in time, when I was more ready to remember, and could accept and cope with what I had become.

In my second book, *Behind Closed Doors* (Thorsons, 1988), I extend that experience to others, reaching out to understand more fully the issues surrounding abuse within the home. The book looks at debt, depression, child abuse, homelessness, second loving relationships, and so on, as well as the abuse and violence which encompasses the whole. All the time, I am searching for the kind of advice and support which might prove useful in encouraging victims today to help themselves.

There are no guidelines to helping a victim of sexual abuse. Sexual abuse can happen to anyone, any time, any place, anywhere. There are no experts; we are still exploring, learning and reaching out for the kind of understanding which we can give to survivors today.

Sexual abuse has been happening since time immemorial. Ignoring the problem isn't going to make it go away. There are no answers; the way to recovery and acceptance is different for everyone. Only if we are prepared to share our experiences, to talk about how we feel, to share our needs, our difficulties, our own way of coping with today, can we at least work together towards a better understanding of sexual abuse as a whole.

There are still gaps in my own memory of past events. I only began to remember enough about my past to write my first book when I married for a second time and gave birth to my first child. People often ask after reading that book why I married Bill. It seems that they can sense the gaps in my memory and need to know everything to understand the whole of my experience.

Early in 1987, I was visiting a maximum security prison, talking to a group of 'lifers', sharing experiences with an openness that made it easy to express ourselves and our feelings. One man, sentenced for murder, with a thirst for the kind of knowledge which would help him to understand his life and crime, stabbed with searching questions, pushing for honesty, for enlightenment of an experience of which he shared no part. In that room, abused and abuser shared.

I have been sexually abused. I was taught to fear sex by my early learning experiences, by my teachers, by my abusers, by my husband, by all those who betrayed my trust.

My first sexual memory is of the boy next door, a year older than me, who pushed his penis between the panels of the garden fence with the challenge, 'I'll show you mine if you'll show me yours'. Curiosity and exploration for a child is a natural part of growing up, but when that initial learning is curtailed by the intrusion of adult phobias based on their own inhibitions of the past, seeing, touching and exploring becomes tainted, cheap, nasty, dirty, abuse.

Somehow, from that point on, I grew up with the idea that naked ness and seeing and touching were taboo. I did not even investigate or explore myself. As I entered adolescence and my periods began, my vagina was so tight that a tampon was pushed out, unable to penetrate the layers of privacy I put between myself and the outside world. Later, I accepted the belief that sex was nasty and hurtful, something which happened to bad girls who didn't know any better. I swamped myself in *Hers* and *Romance* magazines and the idea of love and happy-ever-after endings. I convinced myself that one day my fairy-tale ending would come true. My knight in shining armour would sweep me off my feet, carrying me away to a magical land where nothing bad ever happened to spoil the idyllic dreams of a child.

As a teenager, I was still very naive, vulnerable and innocent. These qualities were obvious to the outside world, and to those who would exploit and poke fun at my expense.

I was born different. My right foot was malformed and I wore calipers and corrective hospital shoes until the age of twelve. At school, I was always different. Children can be very cruel, and I learned to accept that I would be made the butt of their jokes. I knew nothing of the crueller, more callous world of one-parent families, divorce, domestic violence, child abuse and rape, cocooned as I was in a warm, close family of love and laughter, idealism and make-believe. The world outside could be shut out once I returned home.

Yet, already, even at that early age, I was taking on the guilt, the shame, the idea that everything was my fault and that I was somehow attracting negative, depressing thoughts because of the kind of person I had become. At school, different as I was, I yearned to be like others, to be accepted, to be liked for who and what I was outside my home. I didn't trust, so I did not have friends. I was wary of being laughed at and having them turn on me like all the rest. In early teenage years, I tortured myself with cream cakes, punishing myself by eating boxfuls of chocolate, cup cakes and sweets, and then forcing myself to be sick. Already, I was punishing myself for not being the kind of person I wanted to be, for not fitting into a ready mould, and for the dislike and abuse I was attracting from outside. At the same time, I wanted to reach out, to discover what life was really like, held back as I was by the restraints of conditioning and convention.

Soon after my sixteenth birthday, we moved. My father became minister of a new church, and I dreaded the new quest for would-be friends and the ordeal of a new school. I thought I had left schooldays behind. I had taken my exams, gained some 'O' levels, and needed to move on into the adult world where I could leave childhood differences behind. But only the local grammar school offered facilities for furthering my education in music.

Music had become the language of my heart, an escape for the emotion I held hidden from the outside world. Now, because of it, I was again forced back into the classroom. Worse still, I was to be put in a class two years younger than myself so that I could follow my music studies through to the 'O' and 'A' level standard necessary for becoming a teacher. Again, I felt trapped. And yet, I was now so used to doing what I felt other people wanted me to in order to be liked, that it was easy to fall in with their plans.

There were only the two of us taking music. Those classes soon became my escape from the abuse I suffered in other lessons, where chairs were scraped back so that I fell to the floor, where hissing sounded when I walked through the door, where fingers pointed accusingly so that I wondered what I had done. Teachers, unable to control the classroom dissention, looked on while bullies led a full-scale attack on the one they knew to be different. I tried too hard to be liked, to be accepted, to follow their lead. When they pulled back my chair before I sat down, tore up my books, laughed and sniggered and generally waged war on my person, I began spending more and more time absent from the classroom, terrified at the repercussions if I made myself known, closeted in the toilets where I studied alone. My absence made the teachers' job easier, so they did not complain.

The music teacher alone seemed to understand enough to do something about my plight. He was a loner and, like me, music was his salvation. Seeing my unhappiness, he offered his store cupboard as a sanctuary, a haven to hide, to finish my homework, to read, to study, and to work through extra music which I loved. I didn't realize that one day he would seek his reward.

Under the desk, a hand began to search beneath my skirt. While the other music student in my class raced across the staves and dots, his feet beating to the unheard tune in his head, I fought to maintain the privacy I had for so long retained. But the hand was strong, and my denial was weak when I knew what I had to lose. He could close my avenue of escape, and for what seemed a lifetime I would have to suffer the abuse and scorn of my fellow pupils.

The strain was intolerable for a long while. School work suffered because I could not concentrate. At home, I worried myself sick, eating as a combined comfort and punishment. All my life seemed to have been leading to this situation, and I no longer wanted to go on. I thought more than once of ending my life, but even that took courage, and I was not brave.

Finally, the dilemma was resolved for me, or so I thought. The music teacher took me on for private piano lessons at his home and in the classroom he left me alone.

One evening a week, I took a bus ride to his home on the other side of town. At first we concentrated on music for the forthcoming exam. Because of what had happened at school, I felt uneasy in his company. I watched him, distrustful of this new, enlightened relationship between us. My tensions became apparent and my fingers lost their flexibility as they stiffly fell short of the octaves they tried to reach.

He stood behind while I played. Then, with a gentle rubbing of the shoulders, his hands began to knead my neck, brushing my spine. When I hesitated over the next few bars, he nudged me on. I could feel his breath on my neck, his hands, his fingers, touching and holding. My fingers continued their journey clumsily across the keys, while his own rippled up and down my back, caressing, touching, creating a sensation of what would have been calming relaxation if it had not been for the growing knot of dread in my stomach of what else might follow. I was aware of the stillness of the house, the fact that his wife and child were in the far room. All the time he talked, I knew how much depended on this and how pleasant school could be the following week as a result.

Gradually, his presence behind me as I played set a precedent of what would follow. First would come the keyboard practice, my fingers would tense more and more as I felt his hands on my neck and back. Then, gently, he would take hold of the sheet of music before me with one hand, while with the other he led me to the settee behind.

'Please, can't I go on with playing the pieces?' I would plead. 'Let me play the piano. Please? Please, I feel more comfortable on the stool. Here, I feel sick . . .'

His hands would move across to take mine. As he fiddled with the zip on his trousers, my eyes would be mesmerized by his erect penis. Then more often than not, I would tear my hand away.

'No. No! Please don't. I don't want you to make me do that. Can't I just play the piano, that's what I'm here for. Please?'

He would give me a look of rebuke. No more words would be said. He knew I needed him as a friend, an ally. The kind of friends I always had were those who could so easily betray the trust I so readily offered. I was trapped. Next week at school, when the bullies torment and try to find me. . . next week when the teachers cannot stop it happening and I find the chair kicked away from under me, when my books are spoiled, when they corner me in the playground and spit and shout and call me names. . . then I would need the safety of the cupboard in his class where I hide.

His hand positioned mine over his penis, encouraging me to hold and tug, gently up and then down, from side to side. It made me sick. I felt dirty, cheap, used. There was always that look in his eyes which told what would happen if I refused.

I despised *myself* for what *he* made me do. I confronted him, refusing to attend the music lesson at his home, and the following Monday, the door of the music room was locked, shutting me out, hemming me in with the jeering mob who waited outside. All week, it remained closed, and I suffered such abuse from my fellow classmates over the next few days that I could not bear the thought of going in to school.

At the next music lesson, he asked if he should expect me at the planned piano lesson that night, and I agreed to be there. The door of the classroom was open again and my punishment was over. Only when the music exam was over, and I scraped a pass, did I tell him quietly and firmly that I would not be coming back for music lessons.

There is a parallel running alongside this memory, in my experiences with Bill. We met at the church youth club when I was just sixteen, and it was there that he took a bet with his mates about how long it would take to lay the minister's daughter.

I remember the autumn leaves dropping down from the trees like confetti on a newly married couple. This was the first time I had been out with a boy, and I was flattered by his attentions. He liked *me*. He wanted to be with *me*. I didn't know him very well, but I trusted him. By the attention he had lavished on me I knew he could not let me down.

And so it was that we set out to walk alongside the canal, a bag of picnic stuff carried at our side. When he pulled me down under a tree, my only thought was that this was the moment we would eat. I remember reaching into the bag to pull out the bag of sandwiches, laughing as I did so. I felt so happy, and so free.

Then I was falling backwards on to the grass. At first it was a game as I tried to pull myself up, but my arms were pinned to my sides. My head hurt, and I realized that I was being held by my hair. A heavy weight landed on top of me, and then the real fear began.

'Bill? Bill, what are you doing? Let me go, Bill. Bill? Please?'

We were alone. I struggled. I screamed briefly, before a hand clamped over my mouth, blocking out the sound that echoed around my head. I watched the leaves shaking sadly at my dilemma, reaching out, then pointing accusingly as my legs were prised apart and I felt pain like nothing I had ever felt before.

There, on that lonely spot by the canal, I was raped. I learned what sex was all about. And yet, somehow, it did not seem to be any different from what I had expected. Sex was dirty, ugly and shameful, and it hurt like hell. Perhaps this, then, was what I had been guarded against all this time. Sex was separate from love; it held no romance, no illusion. It was painful, brutal; a necessary part of life.

He left me there, bleeding and ashamed. By the time I reached home, I had both accepted and rejected what had happened to me. I carried no memory of it with me into my marriage to Bill five years later, when I moved on to become a battered wife. This, then, was all that I was worth. My trust had been broken a long time since. My feeling of self-worth was zero. I became a puppet on a string, controlled, dominated, obedient to his will.

Rape by the canal built into four-part rape in marriage. He copied what he saw models doing in magazines, smiling as their men climaxed, enjoying the abuse, the bitterness of oral sex. First, he would try to penetrate. My doctor had diagnosed vaginismus, and by this time my vagina walls were so tight as to effectively block him out. He thought I did it on purpose, and fell easily into the role of master, forcing his slave to submit to his will. He tied me, ramming himself where he could do most harm, where he most hurt. Then came the oral sex, knelt at his feet in submission, my head held while he rammed his penis down my throat. Afterwards, he would leave me, humiliated, beaten and abused, while he deserted the scene of his crime.

I am not ashamed of my experiences. The past is a part of me today. It makes me who and what I am. To deny my experience is to deny myself.

This book is about sexual abuse, aimed at sufferers and their families, carers, and professionals. It is for anyone wishing to understand sexual abuse and its effects as a whole. We share the experiences of the children, moving with them into their ongoing suffering as adults today. It is a difficult journey we must follow, but a necessary one if we are fully to appreciate the facts of sexual abuse.

Those who have been abused have a right to be heard. Through sharing our experiences, we aim to offer workable solutions, together with hope and love for those who still suffer today. That which helped us may help you. For carers, there is that chance to learn what it feels like to be one of the abused.

PART ONE
The child betrayed

Dee's experience

Age 0 to 5 years

'The day is warm and sunny. I am being carried around the garden by someone who is big and strong. This same person is talking to me and showing me some flowers. I gaze in wonder at their bright colours, enjoying their sweet perfume. I feel safe and secure.

I am being bounced up and down on a man's knee. He wears a dark suit and he sings to me. I love him very much.

I'm going into a room. Inside is the man I love. I call him grandfather. He asks me to shut the door and I obey. He is sitting down. I go and stand in front of him. His big red face is partly covered with large spectacles, but his eyes are friendly. I go and stand in front of him. He looks so big I can hardly see over his knees as he sits there. Now grandfather is bending over and hugging me, his large hairy hands are going inside my knickers and rubbing me. I feel a new, exciting sensation.

Grandfather has me on his knee. He is kissing me and licking my ears. He has a funny look in his eyes. His hand goes into my knickers. I can feel his finger going up inside me. It hurts, but it's exciting, too. We hear mother coming up the corridor. Grandfather pushes me off for some reason. Mother looks cross, she takes me outside and calls me a naughty girl. I feel confused and sore.

I'm running all over the Vicarage looking for my mother. I want to tell her something important. Something about grandfather. I go to my grandmother in the kitchen and ask where she is. Grandmother says she is lying down. 'Got *another* headache.'

Grandfather has a stained glass window in his study. It's of an angel with a lamb. I look at some of grandfather's books, he has so many. The book cases around the walls are huge and stuffed with old books. He sits down with me and shows me some of the pretty pictures inside. It's so nice when he reads to me.

I'm in the study again with grandfather. He is wearing his usual black suit and white dog collar. Now he puts his hand inside my knickers. The other hand is fiddling with his trouser zip. I don't know what he's doing. I can see something pink that he wants me to hold. He has a funny look in his eyes. 'We must keep it a secret' he says, doing up his zip when mother calls for me. I don't understand secrets.

The day is yellow and dark. Mother calls it London smog. It has a funny taste and it makes me cough if I breathe it in deeply. I am holding mother's hand and walking down the Vicarage drive. I know she is holding my hand, because I can feel it, but I cannot see her properly through the smog. I feel safe knowing she is there. Now she's let go and I feel so alone and frightened. I call 'Mummy!' She grabs my hand again telling me not to be silly as I'm marched off. I don't mean to be silly.

I'm doing a painting. Grandfather and me together. I show it to mother, waiting for her to say it's good. Her face has gone all cross looking. She screws the picture up and smacks me. I just wanted to show her what grandfather and I did.

I'm lying in my bed. It's all dark. Somebody comes in. I don't know who it is. A deep voice whispers, it is my grandfather's voice, his strange one. He takes down my covers and pulls up my nightie. His hands touch me between my legs. It hurts so much. I want to cry, but he puts a finger over my mouth and whispers that it's our special secret and God punishes children who don't keep secrets. I don't know if I'm being loved or punished.

'What is Heaven like?' I ask my grandmother as we walk hand in hand around the sunny Vicarage garden. My grandmother smiles at me. 'Nobody really knows, but we like to think that it's like this garden, full of sunshine and pretty flowers. A beautiful place where you stay forever and ever without any worries.'

'Why do we have to die?' I enquire.

'We can't live forever. When we die and Jesus calls us, we go to Heaven. But only if we've been good.'

'Will I go to Heaven?'

'If you've been good, I hope so.'

I'm sitting in the corner of the room cuddling my knees. I feel horrid because I've been smacked and shaken by my mother.

don't know if I've been sent there or if I put myself in the corner. It feels as if it's a place where I should be, something I deserve.

I'm climbing the cherry tree in the Vicarage garden. I have my old jeans on. Mother doesn't like me in jeans and climbing trees. She says it's not ladylike, but I like climbing trees. I can see the children playing in their gardens behind the Vicarage wall. I wish they would come and talk to me, but I'm too shy to call to them.

Mother likes me to wear pretty dresses when we go out. She always has done. I hate dresses, they are uncomfortable. She says it doesn't matter what they feel like so long as you look nice.

Mother and Father take me into the town to have my hair cut and have my photo taken. Afterwards, we go and have a drink in a restaurant. Mother says I am going to see Father Christmas. She holds my hand and takes me into a dark room where she says Father Christmas is. There are pretty lights and fairies in the room, but it's still dark. Father Christmas looks big and scarey. He wants me to sit on his lap. I start to cry. Mother says not to be silly and takes me out again, back into the light-filled shop. I don't like the dark and big strange men.

It's Christmas Eve and I'm lying in bed in the dark. Mother said that Father Christmas would be coming down the chimney and bringing me presents. I stare at the fireplace in my room. I'm so scared of Father Christmas. He might find me awake in the dark. I want to go to sleep and not wake until he's gone.

Now it's Christmas Day. I can see lots of toys all over my room. There is a doll's cot with a fairy doll inside it. She has a white dress with sequins. She has a sweet smell. The sequins sparkle like magic rainbows. I take her downstairs and put her on the Christmas tree. I like her the best. Lots of aunts come and see us. We sit around the table in my grandparents' dining room and have Christmas dinner. The fire in the grate is warm and comforting. Everyone is smiling and laughing. I do like Christmas Day. I don't want it to end.

I'm starting school today and I am scared. I don't want to leave my mother. There are so many children inside the school, they all look so much bigger than me. I feel so small and insignificant.

Grandfather is taking me to the church cellar to play a game. He opens the door with a rusty old key. With a creak, it opens. I don't like it inside. It smells damp and it's cold and dark. He shuts the door behind us. Grandfather takes my hand and leads me down the concrete steps. I feel unsure, even though he holds my hand.

There is a small, dirty window which lets in a little light, but it just makes everything look more scarey. I can see the large, looming silhouette of a church bell in the middle of the floor. Grandfather says it's a spare one in case the other breaks.

I look around. Beside the steps is a great big pile of coal. Grandfather says it's for heating the church, then he shows me the boiler. He opens the door, the heat that comes out is great and it's all fiery inside.

He leaves the boiler door open, his face looks all red by the heat of the fire and I can see the firelight reflected in his glasses. It makes his eyes look red and wild. Then he holds me by the waist and kisses me on the mouth. That's okay, but then he forces his tongue inside and moves it around. I don't like that way of kissing. His hands are moving all over my body, underneath my dress. It gives a nice sensation. He takes off my knickers, kneels down, and opens my legs. His red tongue starts licking down there, then goes right inside me. It's a nice but funny sensation. It makes me shudder.

Then he stands up and leans against the bell. I can't really see what he's doing, but he calls me over. He makes me hold something warm, which comes out of his trousers. I can't see what it is but it feels the same as the pink thing did in the study. I don't understand it. He tells me to rub it and it goes hard.

I can still see his eyes though, they look all red and frightening. I'm starting to cry. Then I can't, something is in my mouth stopping me. I can hardly breathe. Choking, suffocating, terror.

I can't get away. He's holding me down. Grandfather says I must do it or I'll go into the fire. Something warm and sticky shoots into my mouth and trickles down my throat. Then it's all over, the thing is taken away. I want to be sick, the taste is so awful and my mouth hurts. I want to cry, but he tells me I mustn't.

I don't like these sort of games.

I'm outside now in the bushes, beside the church. Sitting down holding my knees and crying softly, in case he hears me. I feel confused, dirty and horrid. I want to go to my mother, but I am frightened she'll tell me I'm a naughty girl for being dirty. I must be a good girl, I don't want to go into that fiery hell again.

Age 5 to 11 years

It's a lovely hot summer day. I'm standing outside a house and looking down the garden path. Beautiful flowers are growing all over the flower borders and right up to the hedges that surround. It's not my house, but mother says that we will be living there from now on.

She calls me inside and shuts the front door. It's all dark in the hall and smells damp. The stairs are panelled with dark wood. I sit down on the bottom step, I want to go home to grandfather. Mother says 'No, this is our home now.' I start to cry and she tells me off. She says this place is in Sussex and in the country.

I want to go back to London and Grandfather. I feel abandoned.

I've got a new sister now. I don't like her. She cries a lot and everyone runs after her. I want to hit her.

By now, I am nearly seven years old. My father still works in London. On Saturdays and Sundays he stays with Grandfather and Grandmother so he can still get to his band where he is a musician. We don't see him a lot, but he often takes me to stay with my grandparents at weekends. Grandfather still takes me back to the cellar to play games, and to me it is like going into hell, full of terror and pain. He also touches me in his study.

I'm standing by the front door in our house, waiting to go out with mother and Rosemary, my sister. I've a new dress on but it feels so uncomfortable. I won't be able to get hold of my knickers to pull them up. I feel vulnerable.

The classroom is hot. I've got another headache and feel sick. My teacher doesn't like me. She says I'm noisy and don't listen. I can't concentrate anyway. Today my head hurts. It happens often.

It's evening time and I'm in my room. I've been having a bad time at school again. I told my mother and she told me off for not being good. I don't like myself and feel sad.

I'm about seven and a half. I'm in my bedroom and I've found a razor blade. I am cutting my hand. I just feel so angry with myself and the world. Somehow I wish I could change things and make them all right again. I am confused about my feelings and don't know about how I feel inside.

I just want love and attention, but I can't separate it any more from being punished. I know that if I punish and hurt myself I'll get more attention if not love. Maybe I'm not worth loving. I feel disgusted with myself and very guilty.

Dad and I are staying at the Vicarage this weekend. I've gone in to see Grandfather and now I'm sitting on his knee. I ask him if he loves me more than anybody else and he says 'More than anything in the world.' Now he's got his tongue in my ear, it gives me a shivering feeling, all down my spine.

Grandfather is putting his hands down my knickers and is rubbing between my legs. I've got the same exciting feeling that I've had before. It makes me shudder.

Now he has that funny look in his eyes, the one I don't like, and his finger is hurting me as it goes right up inside me, up and down. I feel frightened. It hurts and I don't know why.

Grandfather is making me hold his pink thing and I have to rub it. He says I'll be punished if I don't.

I don't want to go to the cellar. It's all fiery like hell. I'm so very frightened and scared.

Now I'm ten and a half. Mr R from next door has just come round to say he's had a phone call from the hospital. I have another sister now. I wanted a brother.

Aged 11 to 15 years

I've started at Senior School and feel very grown-up. I have two friends. They call me 'Big Dee'. At break times we sit under the tree in the playground, trying to look grown-up. In school, I enjoy writing essays and Art. I like Art and English teachers, they say I'm clever.

Dad and I go for walks together on Sunday afternoons. I enjoy these times, we have fun. I wish, though, that Dad was happier. He tells me he's not and can't talk to Mother. I want to tell him things but find it hard.

Mother is totally wrapped up with my sisters, neither can do wrong. Both seem able to cry to her without being punished. I suppose now that she lives in her own house with her mother to support her she feels happier. As both my sisters have been born here she feels more relaxed having them around. I just remind her of the past and guilty secrets. It isn't so much that I feel jealous of my sisters, more that I feel a great sense of injustice. Why can't I cry without being punished?

I am eleven and my body is beginning to mature. We had lessons about sex at school, but as usual, I haven't been listening, I've been larking and giggling with some friends at the back. Mother has told me a little about periods, but I'm not quite sure why girls get them.

I look at my developing body with some alarm. What is happening to me? Only after seeing some girls in showers at school do I realize I'm not a freak.

Nobody sees me naked. I skip showers with any excuse. I hate my body. Nakedness has never been encouraged in our family. I've never seen my parents undressed.

My periods start, but I don't tell anyone. I just keep wearing and changing many pairs of pants. Somehow it seems just another part of my guilty secret.

I'm twelve years old and the grandmother that lived with us has died. She made slurping noises with her food which reminded me of Grandfather, and the noises he makes when he puts his tongue inside me. It makes me feel uncomfortable and vulnerable, like being subjected to the abuse at each mealtime.

I sit at the table with my knickers up around my chin, continuously adjusting them if they dare move out of place. Rushing down my food just so I can get away fast.

I had managed to keep away from the cellar for quite some time. I'd found a new trick when I went to stay with my grandparents. If I kept away from Grandfather until just after lunch, having made sure that the dishes were safely washed and put away, then Grandmother would go upstairs and get ready to go shopping with me. This gave me just enough time to go and see Grandfather, talk to him and give him a hug, but not enough time to go down to the cellar.

On this particular occasion, in January, a couple of months before my fifteenth birthday, it did happen. Why I let it I don't know, maybe I was desperate for love or I just didn't care any more. I went to his study earlier than usual. He was very pleased to see me, of course. The study looked its normal chaotic self, with books and papers everywhere. I walked over and stood beside a bookcase looking at a photo of my father as a child, when Grandfather came up from behind. At first he put his arms around my waist and told me how very much he loved me. Then his great hands travelled higher, underneath my jumper, until they were firmly clamping my breasts. He started chewing my left ear and whispering 'I'll never leave you, Dee. I'll always be with you.' Then he said something I shall never forgive. 'It would be nice if you could have my baby. Something of me to remember me by.' He was 80 years old.

As his hands travelled down into my pants, I started to protest. He got terribly angry and hit me, then put his hands around my throat, all the time going on and on about eternal damnation if I didn't do as I was told. His eyes looked very evil at that moment.

So I went with him, back to the cellar of Hell. The details of what happened have been completely blanked out of my memory. I can only recall that afterwards, I fought like mad to get away or die in the attempt. I felt death would have been preferable to staying in there with him.

Eventually, I did break free and in a blind cold sweat, stumbled up the steps towards the door and freedom. It seemed to take hours before I could turn the reluctant key and pull open the door. I thought at any minute he'd drag me back in.

The cold, damp brightness made me squint as I rushed outside to safety. Then, like another blow, it hit me, the awful realization that there was nowhere to run to. Where was safe, and what was freedom?

I stared up at the dark old Vicarage that I used to call my home. It seemed to stare back, mocking me. Even the cherry tree outside no longer held any beauty. Its branches were like long dark arms beckoning and waiting to grab me. I wanted to run into my mother's arms, but thought I'd be punished for my wickedness. Maybe if I ran out of the drive and down the street I'd find what? Nothing. Nobody. I couldn't run anywhere. Wasn't he God? He'd find me wherever I went and punish me.

I ran into the bushes, as I'd done as a small child, and sat down hugging my knees, helplessly stuffing the soft material of the skirt into my mouth so no-one would hear me crying. I opened my mouth and wanted to scream, but couldn't make any sound come. Why did God hate me? Why?

Aged 15 to 18 years

It was just after my fifteenth birthday that I thought I was pregnant. Nearly three months had gone by since the incident in the cellar and my periods had stopped completely.

By now, grandfather had been taken into hospital, he'd collapsed one day in the church after suffering a stroke. I was back home in Sussex and hadn't had any contact with him since.

I had a rough idea of how babies were conceived, but hadn't received any definite teaching. Nearly every hour of the day I would rush upstairs and look hopefully for signs of bleeding, but nothing came except increasing desperation.

One frantic day, I asked my mother how you got babies. Her reply was something of a shock and confirmation. 'Sometimes girls get pregnant just by thinking about it', she said. So it was definite then. I'd been thinking, therefore I was. I dashed off to the library to seek further information on symptoms.

Feverishly, I fought my way through a pile of medical books. I found a chapter on pregnancy and there they were in black and white, all my symptoms. Another chapter gave information about abortion and how it was often attempted by other desperate girls: hot baths, alcohol, blows to the abdomen, needles.

I grabbed half a bottle of my father's whisky and leapt upstairs to run a hot bath. It was so hot I could hardly get in, let alone soak myself. The desperation was so bad I just lay back in the water and downed all the whisky.

As I lay there steaming, I wondered what this baby was. Part of grandfather, yes. But a God, or a Satan, or were they both all the same thing? I imagined a great pink monster with horns and terrible eyes nestling in my womb. I thumped my abdomen hard.

The thumps had no effect. No blood, not even a trace. My skin was all red and blotchy from the heat and my stomach was sore, but nothing to suggest a forthcoming abortion.

I was terribly lightheaded and wobbly from all the whisky as I got dressed, but my thoughts were clear. What next? Maybe if I threw myself down the stairs? I'd seen someone do it on a film and they'd lost their baby.

I couldn't pluck up the courage needed to throw myself right from the top, but halfway had to do. With a great crash, I landed on my knees at the bottom. Not what I'd planned. The survival instinct was too great. Still, it was an almighty jolt. Surely this time? Nothing. My knees hurt badly, but that was it.

By now, I was too tired and depressed to do any more, except go to bed and cry. This baby just didn't want to be destroyed. It was my punishment for being wicked.

Over the next few days, I repeated these procedures, until I spent more time in the bathroom than anywhere else. I wanted to speak to someone, but who could I trust?

Then came the knitting needles. I shall never forget this. I found the sharpest one I could find amongst my mother's vast collection and took it back to the bathroom. I stabbed it into myself many times. Each time more violently than before. With a kind of masochistic pleasure and despair, I felt I deserved to feel the white-hot pain.

I stuffed a flannel in my mouth to keep myself from screaming out. I didn't want anyone to hear me. Afterwards, I sat on the toilet sobbing as the first trickle of blood left me.

It was a mixture of indescribable relief intermingled with a terrible fear of forthcoming punishment for having done this. I sat there shaking, expecting any minute to be struck down by the wrath of God Almighty.

Whether or not I had been pregnant I don't know. But over the next few days I lost quite a lot of blood and clots and by the end of the week, felt weak. At least I hadn't been punished for my misdeeds.

One evening, a neighbour came round to tell us he'd received a call that my grandfather had died. We still hadn't got a phone, so urgent messages were passed this way. I went to my room and cried, a little for the love I'd lost, but the greater part for having killed him. Somehow or another, I had killed him. It was all my fault.

That evening, I went out with some friends to a disco, but I couldn't dance. I hadn't even wanted to go, but they'd insisted. I remember sitting there, listening to the Beach Boys 'Darling' and the pretty disco lights flashing around the room, thinking how miserable I felt and how I didn't deserve to be there.

Later that night in my room, I got hold of a rusty old sewing needle and scratched my eyes with it, trying to blind myself. How I hated myself and how disgusted I was with me.

I don't deserve to see any more. I don't deserve to paint pretty pictures. I wish I would go blind. Then the world will know how horrible I am. I hate myself.

I never did go blind, but I had terribly sore and infected eyes for ages afterwards. Mother expressed concern and told me to use my own towel in the bathroom in case I infected anyone else.

The road downhill was approaching fast. I looked okay to the outside world, maybe too good. I had begun dressing in the shortest of skirts and wearing thick, heavy make-up. I went out most evenings with friends, just looking for men. It was the era of the Flower People and 'Peace and Love' was being chanted everywhere. My friends and I would sit on park benches painting flowers on our faces, heaving under the weight of bells and beads dangling around our necks.

I had many one night stands with boys, barely nights, more often an hour or two, just as long as it took to find a quiet spot in the woods, have sex, light a cigarette and kiss goodbye. Quite often, we never got as far as exchanging names. Still, if you chanted 'Peace and love, man' at each other that was more than enough.

Deep down I hated this sort of life. Each boyfriend started off with a separate identity, but as soon as we started making love, he quickly changed to being grandfather and I would start to fight him off. Surprisingly, most boys thought this was part of the game and would want more, but sometimes it frightened them away, being scratched and hit.

There was one boyfriend I was going out with at this time. We went together for several months. No sex, just necking in quiet corners. Then one day, he wanted desperately to make love to me. We were in a field at the time. He chased me round this field with a packet of french letters. I thought it was funny at first, but soon realized he meant business. Then it all became a familiar nightmare. I loved him and didn't want sex to come between us. Sex meant punishment. He caught me and raped me. As I looked at him leaning over me, I could see grandfather with his eyes all red and wild. I hit him and he left me to walk two miles home alone.

I went into a stage of acute depression. My whole family were rowing at this time. I went out to the town and bought two large bottles of aspirin. Life was useless, everyone was punishing me. I had nothing to look forward to and couldn't even go to art school. I felt I hated myself and was locked up in a knot of guilt and didn't know why. About three o'clock the next morning, after a period of crying, I took all the aspirin plus a bottle of migraine tablets, washed down with a glass of tepid water.

I didn't know aspirin made you sick. I was sick and ill. The most appalling ringing in my ears was accompanied by a throbbing headache.

Mother found me in the morning, still vomiting up aspirin all over the place. 'What will the neighbours say?' were her first words to me.

Somebody called an ambulance and I was carted off to hospital, still vomiting. A doctor saw me and gave me a telling off, then I was left alone while he went and spoke to my mother. I lay there crying, crying for having failed, crying for the love I felt I didn't deserve.

A week later, when I was feeling stronger, I announced that I was leaving home. I'd had enough. Mother packed me off to Germany to a family who'd offered me a job as an *au pair*. In her departing speech, she informed me that I'd been booked to see a psychiatrist, but she had cancelled the appointment. I suppose she still didn't want the family name disgraced and her guilt remembered.

How I now wish I had been allowed to go to see the psychiatrist. I was so muddled and confused and so very guilty.

Germany fared about as well as anything else, and within four months I was begging to come home. I'd found a boyfriend out there and was fond of him, but of course, he wanted more so that was that. I vowed I was finished with men forever.

If I can't go to art school, what else do I want to do? Become a nurse. Yes, that's my other dream. I feel I must start to make my own life.

When I got home from Germany, I was determined to make a new start on my own, and I applied to nurse in the Army. But Mother had already written to the local hospital and got me an interview, so I went there. This was going to be a whole new beginning for me. I was going to make a new start to my life.

Dee's experience continues on page 57.

Tina's experience

The first time I was abused was when I was nine years old. I didn't know it was wrong then, although I knew it wasn't right, if you can understand what I mean. It didn't *feel* right to me, and feelings were what it was really all about.

One night, when my mum and sisters were asleep, my dad came into my bedroom. He sat on the bottom of my bed. He told me he loved me. Then he started touching my legs, stroking them up and down. I went to push him away, and he grabbed my legs hard and squeezed them, saying, 'No, Tina. No,' softly but firmly, so that I knew he meant what he said. He started to touch the insides of my legs, moving slowly upwards towards my vagina. He touched my breasts, if you can call them that at that time, and as I again pushed him away, frightened now of what he might do, he warned he would tell if I didn't do what he said.

He climbed on top of me, put my hands behind my head, and held them there while he pushed my legs apart with his and had intercourse with me. When he had ejaculated, he calmly got off, and left my room to go back to his own bed.

I got out of bed, turned on the light, and there was blood all over the sheets. Quietly I went down the stairs with them and washed and dried them clean, putting them back on my bed. In the bathroom, I tried to clean myself up, but the bleeding wouldn't stop. Next day, I got up ready to go to school and I could hardly walk. But I had to act as normally as I could or I might be punished.

When I arrived at school, I told one of the teachers I had been playing on a rail and fallen. They took me up to the hospital and I had to have stitches, but my dad didn't care. That night he was back in my bedroom when the rest of the house was asleep, forcing me to have sex with him. I was scared. I was so scared. I screamed and cried, and tried desparately to push him off and away, but nothing did any good. In the end he had his way, before moving quietly back to his room.

My dad kept on doing this for the next six years. As I got older, I started to understand because of sex education at school. It made me feel so ashamed about what was happening to me and guilty that I might in some way be egging him on. I felt so alone; I just didn't know what to do. I didn't dare tell because of what might happen after. It happened more and more, and now I was really scared of getting pregnant.

I was twelve years old and it was still going on. By now it was almost a nightly occurence. I'd had my periods for almost two years, but my dad didn't seem to give a damn. He still made me have sex with him, and he always had full intercourse.

Then it happened, I found I was pregnant. I went to my aunt's and told her I was pregnant by a boy at school. She took me to the doctor who arranged for me to have an abortion. No one else ever knew. I went in, I came out, and that was that. But inside, I felt such a mess. I was all churned up inside.

One night, I must have been about fifteen, Dad came into my room, and sat on my bed. I leapt up and sat right back into the corner of the headboard. He pulled me down by my legs and said he was going to have oral sex with me. I said, 'No' and kicked him. I tried all sorts that night to make him stop and to get him to go away, to leave me alone, but he wouldn't move. He just kept laughing at me until I spent myself out.

Then he tied my hands behind my back and had oral sex. I was so ashamed, especially when I found myself having an orgasm. This was my dad, not someone who I loved and really cared about in this way! Why me, and why these feelings which should be all about love, real love, love with someone you wanted to be with? I loved my dad, I really did, but not like this.

Not long after, I had a dentist's appointment at the health centre nearby. When I arrived, there was a health visitor there who had been worried about me for some time. She was always asking what was wrong, and was I all right, and could she help? I found her easy to talk to, and this time we met, we chatted over a cup of tea. She kept pressing me to talk about my feelings, about whatever was wrong, to trust her and she would understand.

So I told her. It wasn't easy, it didn't just come spilling out. While one part of me was relieved that someone knew, the other hal of me was wondering what would happen next.

I was very scared. The health visitor phoned a social worker and she told me to go home and say nothing about what had taken place. When I got there, Dad was waiting. I'd been some time, and a dentist's appointment didn't take that long. So where had I been? What had I been doing? Who had I been seeing? What had taken me so long?

I told a load of lies and it all got passed over, and that night the same thing happened all over again. Nothing had changed. I was still there for him.

Next day at school, I was in a child care lesson when the health visitor, a social worker and a policewoman came in, asking to speak to me. The teacher wanted to know what was going on. The class as well as the teacher knew there was something going on, and now that my secret was out I wanted to tell them about it myself.

I was taken with them to the police station where I had to make a statement about what had been happening between me and my dad. My mum and my sister arrived. Mum wouldn't talk about it. At first, she didn't seem to believe me, then she just didn't want to know. She couldn't cope with it all. Later, I found out that my older sister had suffered the same kind of things, maybe that is what kept us close. I find I can talk to her.

Afterwards, there was the internal to go through, which was awful. I said I didn't want to go home, so I went to stay with my older brother for a couple of weeks while my dad was charged.

Tina's experience continues on page 68.

Mary's experience

I remember waking to hear the sound of angry voices shouting at one another, Mum and Dad fighting. Mum used to wind Dad up; She knew how. Dad's mother had had a breakdown when he was only ten or eleven, and Mum would shout at him, 'You're mental, just like your mother!' That used to really hurt my father. Then I'd be down the stairs shouting, 'Stop it! Stop it! Both of you, stop it!'

But there were good memories too in those early days, it wasn't all bad in the beginning. Christmas Eve was always something special. Mum used to do chicken and chips when my grandparents, my father's mother and father, came. I'd lie upstairs, listening to them wrapping the presents up for the next day. They used to have their presents then. They never, ever spent Christmas Day with us, only Christmas Eve. Easter was always indulged. The table would be beautifully laid when we came downstairs, with lovely egg cups with caps on, and loads and loads of easter eggs that would take ages to eat.

Mum used to nurse. She would never be home on time or any thing and she was always having affairs. She was a moody kind of person, always running up bills and things in shops, which my father hated, as he really did work hard.

Then Mum left Dad and I went to live with her. We moved ou of the area. Mum had made friends with a Samaritan, and h helped her a great deal. But only three or four days after moving one of Dad's friends came round. It sickened me then, lying i bed, listening to them both in the next room. I thought, 'Mu can't be bothered that much about leaving Dad. Look at her now And I went down into the kitchen and threatened to take an ove dose of tablets she had in the cupboard. I didn't know what the were, or how much harm they could do. I don't know even if really would have taken them, but at least it stopped Mum and her friend.

Another time when she arranged to meet someone at the house, I made myself sick at school. To me, she was a traitor to my father, and I didn't want it to happen. It wasn't so much that I couldn't come to terms with my mother's sexuality; we had talked, and she said that she had left my father and now had her own life to lead. What disturbed me most was that she wasn't discreet, and exposed us to it all the time, so that it interfered with *my* life. I was the one most sensitive to it, not my brother who would have been 12 or 13 by then, and my sister was too young to know, at three.

Mum started me at a new school in the September of that year, and I loved it. It was small and friendly, everyone knew everyone else, and the teachers had time and space for sensitive beings like me. But then, Mum moved me on to a large, overcrowded school of about two thousand pupils. You could be sitting in a classroom there and never be noticed. I hated it. I felt overwhelmed and lost in a brave new world I didn't know anything about and didn't want to become a part of.

One weekend, Mum was away. We had been left with our grandparents until she returned late on the Sunday night. My school uniform wasn't washed and I had cookery the next day. She just said I would have to buy the cookery things at school, and wear my old uniform in place of the one not yet clean. I said, 'I don't want this. You should be here taking care of us, like any other Mum on a Sunday night.'

She had been out at a party and been wearing a new dress. Grandmother said that it wouldn't be staying on for long, then she went upstairs. That really got to me; it was the end. I said I was going to live with my Dad, and Mum agreed.

She threw all my things together as if they weren't important, and later that night, Dad came to pick me up and I went home. As soon as I got in the car with him, my stomach sank. It wasn't that I wanted to go back, but that I needed things to be different, more how they used to be, the old school where I felt comfortable and safe, our home where Mum and Dad used to live. I wanted it all to go back and to begin over again.

A week later, my brother joined us. Whenever there was an argument Mum used to beat us with a leather belt. When Mum did it to my brother he left and came home too.

Because of the shortage of beds and space where furniture had been moved out, Dad decided I would have to sleep with him while my brother had the other room. It made a certain kind of sense, as two males couldn't sleep together, that just didn't sound right. So it had to be me and Dad. Quite honestly, I believed that it was all right. Mum was taking him to court and I thought maybe he just didn't have the money for beds.

At 12 years old, I didn't even give it a second thought, climbing into my father's bed. Initially, Dad would always have the tea ready when we came home from school. But then gradually, I took on more and more work around the house. It became too much by the time I was 14, with school as well and the sexual activity which had crept in between.

It was February, 1974. My first and second years in secondary school seemed to disappear. I can remember little things, like the social worker visiting the house because my Mum was by now accusing Dad of being an alcoholic. He came regularly in the beginning to see that we were all right and feeling happy about things, although he never went upstairs to check the sleeping arrangements.

We helped Dad strip the living room and decorate. Decorating my old room was an excuse he seemed to use to keep me in his bed. 'Decorate it, decorate it', he used to say. But then we never had the money, and the job kept getting put off and put off until it just never happened at all.

Dad had a girlfriend for a while, and when she stayed, I went back into my own bedroom. Mum sent over a bed and a few odds and ends for me. I can remember saying that we would be able to share the old kind of Christmasses again now that she was in the house.

Grandad died in the same year. He came to stay at the house for a while too, sleeping downstairs. He'd had a stroke, and couldn't do things for himself. I had to bath and feed him. He was incontinent. He needed me and what little I could offer then.

When Grandad died, I helped Dad clear out his home. We had his Christmas tree that year, and I can remember the furniture that we had for ourselves. Dad had several girlfriends then, and when they went home, Dad would come and get me out of my bed to spend the night with him. I remember one girlfriend had the most sweaty feet. When I went into the big bed, the bedsheets used to smell of these feet. It was the most horrible smell and it made me feel really really sick.

In the beginning, I would go to bed with Dad at the same time. One night, I went out with a school friend and, collecting a bag of chips on the way home, I arrived back at nine o'clock instead of eight. Dad was so drunk and so loud and he battered me so much. That night, I lay in my bed, my own bed, really shaking.

When I went to bed with Dad, I used to wear this nightdress, which was bought for me for the times I went to hospital. It was really pretty, coming right down to my ankles. Underneath, I used to keep my pants on. My father would cuddle up to me. Then his hands would touch my breasts and I would push him away.

After I'd fallen asleep, I'd wake up to find his fingers inside me. Again, I'd push him away and pull my knickers back up. Sometimes it would frighten me because I'd sleep through it, or else my subconscious would block it out. In the morning, I'd find I had no pants on at all. Something more happened in the night that I didn't know anything about.

I never really acknowledged what was going on, but I would pull my nightdress close in around me, right in to the backs of my legs, so tightly that I could reassure myself that nothing like that could happen while I was asleep. In the morning, the buttons on my nightdress would be open, evidence that something had happened that I didn't know about. Then I'd be washing myself and I'd find bites on me, bites on my breasts. And it just progressed from there, it just got worse and worse and worse.

I would have been about 12 or 13 when one night I was asleep, and thought I was dreaming. My father was having oral sex with me, and I climaxed. At the point I reached the climax, I pulled my father on top of me and he went inside, and I realized that I was enjoying it. I actually enjoyed what was happening to me and the feeling it gave me after it was done.

I kissed him. And the memory of that kiss, and that night, and what we were doing makes me feel so so bad. I shouldn't have enjoyed it. I shouldn't have let it happen. It made me bad, made me a part of that crime, his crime. And yet what could I do? I was a child in his care. My body responded to his attentions. It became a need, my need. The kind of need which had to be fed and which I could do nothing about.

After that, I took on board all the guilt, the shame, the fear. I stopped pushing him away, and began to think if we just got on with it, then he'd leave me alone. We never talked about it, and he never said anything to me, except that we shared a special kind of relationship, and if I ever left home, or there was ever any trouble, then he would deny it. It just wouldn't have taken place.

Mary's experience continues on page 70.

Sue's experience

My life didn't start until I was ten. Then there was Mum and me...and Dad. He was always there. He wouldn't leave me alone.

One day, the school arranged that I went to see a psychiatrist. I couldn't concentrate on my work, I was always tired and kind of dreamy, as if I didn't really belong in class. I would be crying and not be able to tell them what it was all about. I carried around a dark and lonely secret that I could not share. I didn't dare. And so I had to find a way of coping with it on my own.

I dreaded going home at the end of a school day, and when people began to notice and there was the danger that this dreadful secret could come out, I played truant.

The day I visited the psychiatrist it all came out, like emotional diarrhoea. I rid myself of all the pain, the hurt, the shame, the dirt, the confusion, the guilt that it was somehow all my fault which I had built up over the years. It was such a relief. Someone was listening, someone was willing to do something and this someone would take all my hurt away.

I'd tried to commit suicide, to end it all more than once because no one seemed to care, to understand about what was happening to me. I was just a child, a minor. I didn't have a voice. But now, it was going to be different. The psychiatrist would make it so. She listened. She seemed to understand. And as I unloaded everything I had been carrying around for so long, I began to trust.

At the end of the session, I remember slumping back in the chair, drained and spent. I waited to hear what she would say. I trusted her. I knew she was going to end what was happening to me and make my life better again.

The psychiatrist leaned across the desk and picked up the phone. I saw her dial a number, then I heard her speak to my father, asking him to make an appointment to come in and talk. Even from where I was sitting, I could hear my father's growl, 'Why?' my father demanded. 'What is going on? What's it all about?' The psychiatrist told him there and then, over the phone, most of what I had told her. And when my father heard, he told her that I was the one who was mad. I was the problem. I should be locked away, making up stories like that. I was sick.

The psychiatrist sent me home. She said there wasn't anything else she could do. It was his word against mine. Later, a social worker came around to talk to my mother about taking me into care. But why me? Why send me away? I hadn't done anything wrong. Or had I? Maybe it *was* me. Maybe it was all my fault. And yet, I didn't know what it was I was doing that was so awful, so wrong.

A few days later I ran away. The police would find me sleeping rough, on park benches, in railway stations, at bus terminals. Because I was a minor, no matter what I said, the police would take me home.

I moved further and further away, hitching lifts from all-night lorry drivers, and finally, I stayed away for good. The police weren't going to find me to send me back. In the end, my parents gave up reporting me missing and began to get on with their lives. My dad was still there, ready to do as he pleased with me. For me, there was no escape. I'd feel so used, so dirty, so ashamed of what *he* was doing to *me*. Anything was better than that. On the streets became safer than living inside my home.

Sue's experience continues on page 76.

Jane's experience

I am ugly. I have always been ugly. My mother tried to have an illegal abortion when expecting me, but it failed. It made her ill, so she blamed me. She always said I wasn't good for anything. Sometimes she told me I was born evil and rotten.

My dad always said I wasn't his, they all have blue eyes and mine are green. I was a quiet, shy child, which was my big fault and made me stand out as being different because they were very outgoing and extrovert people.

Everything before the age of six is a bit of a blur in my memory, not very happy, but okayish. When I was five, my sister was born, pretty, cute, a real doll. She got toys I had only dreamed about, though I didn't and don't resent her.

My dad used to beat us every Sunday. He said it would do us good. Then, when I was six, we moved to a bigger and better house with a large garden. It wasn't a bad place. It was then that someone started to hurt me, someone 12 years older than me. He tied me up, hit and sometimes cut me. He'd wanted to be a knife thrower once so I guess he used me as a target. He would put out his cigars on my thighs and tummy, every Wednesday and Monday afternoons, which were his half-days.

From about seven up until I was 13, my mother said it amused him and kept him out of her way. Once, I hung on to the door downstairs, screaming. She hit my fingers until I let go, and then he took me upstairs. Mum said I was ungrateful. Dad said I was wicked and deserved all I got. He would put things inside me, usually until I bled. It was so violent, and writing this even now makes me feel sick. I still have scars on my wrists where the string cut in.

When I was nine, the sex started. I struggled a lot so he used to squeeze my throat till I passed out. He used to say he would kill me if I tried to stop him. Then when he realized I wanted him to kill me to make the pain go away, he threatened he would hurt my other brother. That meant I had to take my love away so that my brother would not get hurt.

He used a long rubber hose to blow in me. I didn't feel pain after a while. He said he did it because I was so ugly, and that I wouldn't get attention any other way. He liked to see blood, and I bled a lot. Besides, as my mother said, it kept him quiet.

It's only me. That's what they used to say. She doesn't count. Fit for nothing, that's me. Stupid, thick, hateful, nasty, bitchy, disgusting. Some people don't deserve to live, do they? Why couldn't he have killed me then? I wouldn't have minded really. At least it would have stopped the pain.

Jane's experience continues on page 78.

Understanding the sufferer

To be touched sexually by an adult when you are a child is sexual abuse. It is a betrayal of trust, a betrayal which hurts just as much if it only happens once as if it happens all your life.

Child sexual abuse is committed in every class, race, religion, cultural and ethnic group. It is not a crime of the dangerous stranger, but committed more often by someone the child trusts and loves. Many times, the offender perpetuates the abuse by preying upon the child's innocence, confusion, dependence, guilt and fear.

Only a proportion of abused children will have outward signs of the distress they suffer within. The abuser may lead up to inappropiate fondling by tucking the child into bed or giving a bath, a hug, a rub. Each act seemingly innocent and free from abuse. At first, the abused may not even be aware that something is wrong.

Children then become vulnerable because they have no self-awareness of their growing bodies, and 'good' and 'bad' touches. So when those hugs or rubs or cuddles begin to make them feel uncomfortable they will not know how to deal with the situation enough to say 'no'. As abuse continues, they will have no conception of how to make it stop, or how to tell someone what is happening to them.

Abused children will feel confused. Their sense of betrayal will be very strong. Someone they once trusted is now hurting and destroying their trust, and their love. As such, they will feel vulnerable, isolated, insecure and alone. Who is there now for them? Who can they talk to? Where can they hide? How can they take away the hurt that is twisting them up into a knot of tension, fear and dread? And if they were to talk about it, how could they find the words outside the emotion to express how they now feel inside?

Sexual abuse, if forced to become an established pattern in their lives, will bring into play a whole new set of feelings which they cannot cope with on their own. Their sense of normality will adjust accordingly as they try to take on board new modes of behaviour and new rules by which to live their lives. Unintentionally, they will give off strong sexual vibrations and begin to attract the same kind of abuse happening elsewhere, from people already a risk. They will act out what they have been taught, the look, the moves, the positions. Thus it becomes easy for them to maintain their belief that it is somehow their fault, that they are to blame. The tremendous sense of guilt will remain with them for as long as they are without the necessary counselling and support and help they so desperately need to reassert themselves as normal caring human beings.

If, in the future, abuse is then suddenly taken away, they will suffer withdrawal symptoms which will make them feel rejected and abandoned, cut off from those new sexual experiences which have become an integral part of their lives. Again, they will take that guilt upon themselves as being directly responsible for the outcome, a punishment for the kind of people they have become.

Because of the betrayal, an abused child's mistrust of one adult will extend to all adults both inside and outside the home. Within themselves, they will feel so hurt at what is happening that it will take over their thoughts and feelings so completely as to make concentration elsewhere impossible. At school, they will be high-lighted as unruly and disruptive children in class, unable to concentrate on lessons, frequently disobedient, unable to produce homework on time. Truancy may be rife. They may suffer from nervous complaints, and when the strain of pretence becomes too great, take to running away, or in the extreme, try to take their life through suicide, so depressed and confused will they have become.

Since a young child will find difficulty in verbalizing his or her fears about what is happening to them, the signs to look for are likely to be physical and behavioural.

- Bedwetting

- Severe nightmares

- Explicit knowledge of sexual parts

- Knowledge of or interest in sexual acts inappropriate to the child's age
- Acting out of adult sexual behaviour
- Unwillingness to undress
- Avoidance of touch
- Excessive masturbation
- Constant need for love and affection and/or clinging
- Unwillingness to go home
- Truancy from school
- Lack of concentration
- Food disorders, such as anorexic or bulimic tendencies
- Constant anxiety
- Sudden changes in personality and mood swings, withdrawal or regression
- Constant crying without any reason.

In the older child, teenage sons and daughters may

- Be depressed
- Be secretive
- Be seductive, using body-language with companions of the opposite sex
- Be suicidal
- Have low self-esteem
- Run away from home
- Use alcohol/drugs or binge on sweets/chocolate
- Use self-punishment by scratching or cutting themselves, or burning themselves with cigarettes.

It should be noted however, that many of these signs can also be symptoms of different forms of distress. If parents learn what to look for and educate themselves about child behaviour and sexual abuse, these signs will be noticed as they occur. And it is worth being aware that abuse could be a cause.

Revealing sexual abuse can be a major trauma for the child. It becomes their well-guarded secret. Confrontation by an adult will give rise only to further confusion for the abused as they sense that their loyalty is being questioned, and loyalty towards an abuser can be strong, as it is the abuser who has control. A child will test that confronting person's level of belief and reaction accordingly, very often with an outright lie, keeping their guilty secret to themselves, too afraid of the consequences to speak the truth. Often they are under threat from their abuser. They may have been told that telling will mean they will be sent away to a place for bad children, or that their best friend or pet will be hurt or killed.

Sadly, the fear of what will happen if they tell will be so great as to prevent them maybe ever sharing their experience fully until adulthood when it is too late to directly intervene and stop the kind of problems they will inevitably suffer from in later life.

The first thing to do if you are a victim of sexual abuse is to admit to yourself that you have a problem. That problem isn't simply going to disappear. Nor can you deal with it on your own. But you do have to do something about it to help yourself. Telling someone whom you trust is the first, most important step. And telling the right person will dictate what will happen next. For a child it will be like breaking an unwritten law, and extremely painful and daunting.

If a child self-discloses, it is essential that the listener expresses no disbelief or shock. Children do not lie about sexual abuse. They have probably taken a long time leading up to this moment. They will probably feel more vulnerable now than at any other time. They will be watching for reaction, wary of being betrayed again.

The listening adult should then help the child to confide, to assure him or her that what they have done in talking about their abuse has been the right thing to do, and that they will not be punished because of it. The child needs to know above all that what he or she says is confidential. The most difficult time will be supporting him or her whilst working towards that point where you can go together through relevant channels, so that the necessary change will be brought about in order for abuse to stop.

The abused does not necessarily want the abuser punished. The abused may also be frightened that they will be sent away. What they will want more than anything will be for the family to live together happily and without abuse. But this may not be possible. The child will need a great deal of tender loving care to help him or her through the ordeal of what is to come when the abuse is finally dealt with outside the family home.

For the steps needed to confront sexual abuse and reporting it to the relevant authorities, read Michele Elliott's book *Keeping Safe: A practical guide to talking with children* (Bedford Square Press, 1972).

It takes courage to talk about sexual abuse. Understanding what has happened to you, the abused, is vital. You need to read as much as possible (see Bibliography, p. 200 for books which may be helpful) to understand the subject as a whole. There has also been an increase in media information about sexual abuse which may be helpful. Watching television programmes and reading about abuse may be painful, but at those points where you stop and cannot go on, ask yourself why. Find out about your fears, and confront them. Be prepared to help yourself. You know more about your experience and the feelings you have been left with than anyone else. Learn about yourself and how to cope in the aftermath of abuse.

There are also children's books aimed at putting across the idea of danger within the home and from people they may know, in a simple yet effective manner. See the Bibliography (p. 200) for further reading. You may find the content of some of the books disturbing or distressing. Never be afraid to stop reading or listening or looking when you feel you have had enough, but note the bits you feel most upset about, as they will probably be most relevant to you.

One of the biggest steps you will take is accepting that what happened was not your fault. This seems very simple, so simple that many people who have not been abused look on it as an obvious fact and omit to explain it to children who have been abused. To a victim of sexual abuse, the feeling of total responsibility is such an integral part of their personality that is hard to let go. Intellectually, many adults agree quite easily when it is pointed out to them that the abuser was an adult and you, the abused, were a child. It is emotionally that victims of abuse have trouble accepting this.

One of the things you can do to help put this problem in perspective is to consider other people in that position. If, for example, you were abused when you were eight, look at eight-year-olds around. See how childlike even 13-14- and 15-year-olds are, mostly playing at being adult in preparation for their real life roles, still children in need of care and protection. Look at the reasons you think it is your fault.

● I led him on

● It was the way I smiled at him

● I could have told someone

● I felt sorry for him

● I took sweets/money/toys from him

● I enjoyed it.

What all these statements overlook is the total selfishness of all abusers who don't care how their victims think or feel. All the abuser wants is sex at any price without any thought for the consequences. It is the adult's responsibility not to betray the child's trust.

Sexual pleasure is a very natural part of a human being's make-up. Children touch themselves and each other as a normal part of growing up, but if a child has been sexually abused by an adult, they may become very sexually aware. This is conditioning and nothing to do with wanting sex. Many children respond to sexual stimulus, not realizing that this is beyond their control. Their guilt is further compounded by the abuser using the situation to shift the blame on the child, by saying something like, 'You responded so you must have wanted it.' The child is left feeling that they have even been betrayed by their own bodies. This is the secret heart of child sexual abuse and understanding it is another step towards accepting that it is *not* your fault.

Abused children have had their innocence cruelly taken away and they are brought into conflict with an adult world in which, by right, they should have no part. Their innocence is touched by a sense of shame at the kind of people they have become. Often, by the time they find some way of relating to their problem they just want to forget their past and get on with the rest of their life. They begin to suppress their emotions, running away from the facts or dismissing them with phrases such as 'it wasn't much', 'it only happened once', or 'it was only touching'.

There is no such thing as 'only touching'. To be touched sexually by an adult when you are a child is a *betrayal of trust* — a betrayal which hurts just as much if it only happens once as if it happens all your life. You cannot quantify.

Education has to begin at home. As a means of prevention, it is important for every child to learn to say *no* to sexual advances as part of their learning for life. Sexual abuse may never happen to your child, but at least we can be prepared.

Streetproof your children

Helpful rules to keep young people safe

Most parents want to educate their children about sexual abuse, but they don't know how. These guidelines will help parents to teach their children how to keep safe. Remember, you can't tell a child too much; knowledge doesn't stimulate inappropriate behaviour, ignorance does. Parents who talk openly with their children will be 'askable' parents, and children will feel free to bring their worries and concerns to them in the future.

- An unattended child is a child at risk. Arrange, with your child, an alternative place to wait if you are delayed, especially in the darker winter evenings. Suggest a well-lit store or school

- Always, where possible, have children walk in pairs or groups

- Children should always travel the same way home

- Use a secret family code. Children should never go with anyone, not even a close family friend, unless they are able to give a child the code. Once the code has been used, it should be changed

- Don't allow your young child to go to a public washroom unattended

- Check your babysitter's credentials thoroughly. In your absence they are guardian of your child

- Tell your child it is not rude to ignore an adult who is asking directions on the street. Another adult could be asked for more accurate directions

- Tackle the subject of sexual abuse prevention with the same honest, matter-of-fact manner you would attach to road safety. Remember, the only time a child will ask you about sexual abuse is after it has happened. Open the subject and your child will remember that you are askable

● Discuss with your child the difference between fact and fancy, fact and fiction, so that they may understand the nature of taking an oath. This may be necessary for a court appearance

● If you suspect that an abuse has taken place

a) *Do* encourage the child to talk about it

b) *Do* establish in the child's mind that they are not to blame

c) *Do not* correct the child's story. Listen to the original words, even those which are babyish or family words

d) *Do not* suggest or modify what the child is trying to say. Your ideas might confuse the truth

e) *Do not* show horror or anger. However, if caught by surprise and unable to control your emotions, be clear that your anger is meant for the offender, not the child.

The above is taken from a *Childwatch* leaflet which comes with their information pack, price 65p. Their address is in the Directory of Advisory Services in the UK (p 171) at the back of the book.

PART TWO
The woman survivor

'There is no past. Past is present when you carry it with you.'
Flora Rheta Schreiber

Dee

I feel so awful, so sick all the time, so vulnerable and hurt inside, like a lost and lonely child. I have given custody of my three children to my ex-husband. I am finding it hard to cope.

My daughter, Lisa, has been in danger from me since she was two years old. She reminded me of myself as a child and everything I was taught to hate. She reminded me of my grandfather who used to abuse me. I tried to be kind by getting her things, but it was all on the surface. I've bought her things, clothes, a pet rabbit, but it's all to replace the fact that I can't cuddle her or love her. She and I would battle our way through the days. It was bad. If I didn't punish her, I punished myself. I wish I knew who we were, where one ended and the other began. We are so alike, punishing her is the same as punishing me. I've told myself she's not me, but then have punished myself more.

I do not love her, yet I *do* care, I care that I might hurt her. I see her as being me, hurting her would be a form of suicide, it would destroy us both. Deep down I feel she deserves to be loved, she gets on well, all three get on well with my ex-husband, so they have all to go to him. I feel guilty, awful, I can't begin to describe how I feel.

I have made contact with Bristol Incest Crisis and they want me to see a psychologist. The NSPCC already know me, but can't do anything because I am in contact with Social Services. The Social Services also want me to see a psychologist on the NHS, but one hasn't been appointed to this area yet. In the meantime they say I must wait. I must somehow get through on my own.

When my children were at home, my social worker would say I ought to get a job, meet 'normal people'. Family therapy wouldn't help, they said, but in the meantime, if I hurt Lisa they'd all be taken away. I felt an immense pressure I couldn't cope with to keep control. It was like being transported back some 30 years. Lisa became me, and no one seemed to want to know or to care enough to do something positive to help. In the end, the only way out seemed to be to give up my children. Having done that, they leave me alone. I exist.

Now I feel I have nothing left to live for. I have switched off emotionally, and it's hard to concentrate like this. I do not feel happy or sad. I simply don't feel. I'm not sure whether it is self-preservation or whether it's destruction. All I know is that I hear voices saying 'help me'. One is mine and the others belong to something or someone trapped. I hate the nightmares and I hate being alone. The little part of me that wants help and is seeking it is being drowned by my grandfather and the child who knows she doesn't deserve love or help of any kind. I'm trying to keep them at bay, but they take over so often and push me aside and that's when I lose control and do things. I am scared to express myself in case *he* gets me. My grandfather is still very real despite the number of years he has now been dead. He is still punishing me for everything, and he punishes and hurts all those with whom I come into contact.

I feel perhaps now, without my children, that I must find the true me. Maybe then I can start liking myself and therefore start liking my daughter. One day the children may want to come back. I feel rejected and unloveable. There are tears I cannot shed. The other day I sat in a corner hugging my knees, just as I did as a child after the abuse. I find it hard to cry, but I want to so badly. I need to cry now, but I've had so many years of practice at keeping tears at bay, it's so very hard to unlearn.

My husband didn't abuse me. He just didn't understand. It was easier for him to believe I made up stories about my past than to have to deal with the reality of who I had become. Towards the end it was as if he had turned into my grandfather. Our lovemaking turned into vicious fights; I thought he was abusing me. I never enjoyed making love, not ever. Maybe I was the one who was abusing him. He would never talk to me about it or recognize it for the problem it was. We couldn't communicate enough to share problems and thoughts.

I feel scared of being alone, of punishment. Through the years I have been mutilating myself physically, cutting myself with glass, scratching myself. Deep down I feel it's my grandfather. He was a vicar and was always going on about punishment, hell and damnation. I still feel he is punishing me, though I try to tell myself he's not, that it's me.

I began going to counselling at an independent counselling service. It's about the hardest, worst thing I have had to do, but necessary, I suppose. To go through it made me feel suicidal, and this happened every week. I still hear voices most of the time telling me to do things, or torturing figures leaping at me. My counsellor thought there may have been black magic involved in my childhood and this is what's destroying me inside. After my last counselling session, I took drink and Panadol and anything else I could find to dull the pain so I wouldn't hear those awful voices calling, 'kill, hate, destroy'. I found it took several days to come back to the present, but even then I was haunted, and very self-destructive.

More recently, I went to see my parents, trying to tell Mum for the first time what happened to me as a child, and why I took my first overdose at 16. The BBC programme *Childwatch* gave me the courage to do that. I was in London to do a recording for the programme with Esther Rantzen, and I thought it was a suitable time to talk to Mum. She couldn't accept what I said, more or less passing the buck. 'Leave it to your counsellors, dear. Leave it to them,' was all she would say. She did tell me certain things that happened to Dad which helped me make sense out of the situation. He'd had psychological problems all his life, seeing psychologists and psychiatrists, but no one ever seemed to get to the bottom of his problem. It was something never talked about at home. I think now that he was abused by his father as a child, my grandfather, my own abuser, and he was never given a chance to talk about or get over it.

I came away from there feeling that she was telling me she had enough to cope with with him. 'I can't cope with you as well. Don't tell me this.' So I came back from that weekend feeling I'd got to stay up. I was trying really hard, making cushions, sewing and things, keeping myself busy, and my thoughts occupied, but I kept losing concentration. I was still going to counselling once a week for an hour, but it wasn't enough. I just couldn't cope with the flood of feeling it produced when I got back.

I didn't find the counselling helped at all. She would put the clock on as soon as I came through the door, and exactly an hour

later, that was it. Time's up. Off you go. The sessions had no struc-
ture or format. I never knew what we would be talking about from
one week to the next. She'd say we would talk about such and
such a thing, and I'd get all keyed up for it. Then when next week
came, we'd talk about something else, something completely different. There were so many things that came from my past which
seemed to lead up to the present and my feelings now, needing
to be talked about. But it was very much the attitude 'don't drag
in the past. Let's cope with the present.' But then they never taught
me how to cope, and afterwards I would feel so helpless, and alone.
I became overwhelmed with frustration and anger. I felt unable
to go on.

When I used to say to her, 'Look, I've got all these angry feelings. I can't cope,' she'd say, 'Well recognize these feelings. Say to
yourself, that's a nasty feeling. Then go and do something positive. Go shopping or something. Buy a cake.' I thought, 'But that's
not dealing with it, that's pushing it aside, putting it off until later,'
and later never comes.

In October I appeared in the BBC *Childwatch* programme. That
brought it all back and was difficult to handle afterwards. When
it was broadcast I was staying at my ex-husband's looking after
the children during half-term. I hoped that if he and my elder
son watched it with me it would help them understand how I
felt, and why all this was happening to me. He didn't want to watch
it. He fell asleep for the first part, and for the second he had a
bath and went to bed. I was left with the lodger and my son, and
as soon as it finished they both went off to bed. I was alone, and
that was when everything sort of exploded in my head. I couldn't
cope; I felt I was going mad.

The following week I went home to my regular weekly counselling session and told her how I felt. She just said, 'But Dee,
you've got to cope with these bad feelings. You've got to cope.
You've *got* to cope.' But she never told me how. She kept looking
at the cuts and scratches on my face and my arms, my way
of punishing myself. 'They're getting worse, aren't they?' she
said. 'I've been watching you going downhill for the last few
weeks. But you've got to cope. I think you ought to see the
psychiatrist.' But how am I supposed to contact the psychiatrist?
'Oh I'll contact him for you, and I'll contact your social worker.'
I thought, 'At last something's being done!' But then that was the

last I heard. Nobody contacted me at all.

I shut myself away indoors for a month. I didn't want to see anyone. And yet at the same time, I did. I wanted someone to come round to see why I hadn't appeared since I went to see the children. I stopped going to counselling, I just wasn't getting anywhere. She was bringing out things I didn't know how to cope with, and she wasn't teaching me how to cope. I was getting more and more cut and scratched up, more and more desperate.

I hadn't been coping with food for a long time. Since the summer, I'd be sick after I had eaten, then binge, then be sick. It was my way of coping with an intolerable situation. Making myself sick seemed to relieve stress. I wasn't eating the right things at all. I was living on cakes, or a bit of bread. Now and then I'd have a tin of soup, but then that would last me all the following week. I remember one day sitting on the floor in the dark eating meat straight out of the freezer. I was living like an animal. I continued living this way for a whole month.

In August, when I last saw my social worker, she said she would come to see me again in October. Then she phoned to say she couldn't come. She was going on three weeks' holiday. 'I'll come and see you when I get back.' I thought, 'Fair enough. I'll try and hang on for those three weeks and I'll see her on her return.' She didn't make a home visit again.

On Monday 24 November, a letter arrived saying she understood I was ill. She had contacted the psychiatrist and my counsellor. 'If I can be of any further assistance in the future then please feel free to contact me.' It felt like a write-off, and that was the last straw as far as I was concerned. She wasn't coming. I was feeling so ill. I went wandering, and luckily a friend found me. 'I don't know which way the town is' I was saying. 'Where am I?' I just didn't know where I was or what I was doing any more.

I'd been told by my counsellor that the way I was coping wasn't right, yet I didn't have an alternative. My eating habits were more peculiar, more bizarre, and I was cutting myself with glass, knives, anything that was sharp, trying to cut out the feelings inside. I kept it dark at home with the curtains drawn, all the time feeling so physically sick and ill.

On this Monday after the letter came, I thought, 'I feel so hungry. I must go and get something to eat, the only thing I can cope with is cake. Let's go to town. I'll never get on the bike and arrive there in one piece. It's too much!' This is when I drifted into my friend. She took me to town and I got a cake in a cafe. I kept saying I had to see the social worker; she seemed to be my only hope. Someone who would perhaps talk to me, tell me what to do, someone to get things done. I didn't want to go into hospital, I just wanted someone to come and give me practical help in the house, someone to talk to and who would listen. By this time I had just about wrecked my home.

My friend took me up to the social worker, but I wouldn't go in, I wanted her to come to me. My friend went in to see her and the social worker advised my friend to take me up to the hospital. She wouldn't come out, she wouldn't see me. I ended up in casualty, my GP shouting at me, telling me off, telling me not to be so stupid, telling me to turn round and face him when he spoke. 'Look at me when I'm speaking to you!' I curled up in a heap in the corner of the room and switched off. 'Oh well, if that's how you're going to be, I've got other patients to see. I'll come back and see you later.' He spoke to my friend and she told him what she thought about the state in which I was living. Then he said finally, 'I'll admit her to hospital', and walked off.

I waited around in casualty, where a hospital driver came and took me to the mental hospital with a letter from my doctor stating I had a 'known hysterical personality disorder. She says she has been hearing voices and has been trying to get the evil out of her. She's either got a psychotic illness or else she's being hysterical.' I thought, 'But I'm neither of those things. It's just that I haven't been getting the right kind of help. I can't talk about my past and I don't know how to cope, that's all. I've just gone over the top.'

On the journey to hospital, I remained curled up in a corner of the car, totally switched off to what was going on around me. From that moment on, I can only remember bits of what happened during the two months I spent in hospital.

The day after I was admitted, my friend brought me some belongings, which were promptly taken away. People talked to me on and off, but I still felt that I was very much being left to cope. I kept trying to cope, I really did. I went away into little corners hiding, and had to be pulled out. 'No, you know you shouldn't be in this cold corner. You shouldn't be doing this. You shouldn't be doing that,' the nurses said. I kept going back to bed, then into

the corner. 'You must be with us, you must socialize.' But everything seemed so bright, so noisy, all these people making so much
noise. Again, I was desperate. Again there was nothing structured
about what was happening to me. I became very depressed.

One night I slashed my neck. After I'd done it, I crawled away
into a cupboard, and I was just sitting there when they pulled
me out. 'Look at this! She's got a deep cut on her neck.' The next
day, nothing was really done about it, except that they were watching me. They couldn't have been watching me that well because
I wandered outside, and ended up sitting in the dark, huddled
in the yard. Someone came out and saw me and I was taken in
and ushered into the lock-up ward. That was terrible. There were
people there who were really disturbed, noisy, stamping up and
down, banging their heads. I felt like I was in prison, being
punished.

That Thursday evening, I became hysterical because I thought
I was being punished for doing something bad. I knew something
had to be done. I was so thirsty. I asked if I could have a drink.
I said, 'Please can I have a hot drink or something? It would calm
me down.' This male nurse just shouted at me. 'Look, I'll take you
along and show you the rules. This is when you can have a drink.
You can have as much as you like to drink at mealtimes, but in
between you drink water.' I was getting more and more hysterical.
I shoved off into a corner, and again the male nurse shouted and
pulled me out. It was a good job that one of the student nurses
was allocated to me. She was the only one who was nice, talking
to me, keeping me calm.

I stayed in the lock-up ward for ten days.

Everything that happened is like some terrible nightmare. When
returned to my usual ward, the nurses and patients had changed.
Now it was all male nurses and patients. Nobody really wanted
to talk. I used to go and lie on the bed. Sometimes, I would go
downstairs, but only if it felt safe. With so many male nurses and
patients, I felt threatened and stayed on my bed.

At night we had sleeping tablets. There was no other form of
tablets or set counselling. Only two or three times over my stay
did I get to talk to a staff nurse in a side room. The rest of the
time staff were too busy as several older patients were admitted
who needed a lot of attention. I shut myself off, trying to cope
the only way I knew how on my own.

The week before Christmas there were male nurses on in the evening. I'd been in the dormitory on my own as a lot of patients had gone home for Christmas. It was dark and I was too scared to go downstairs with male nurses and patients wandering around. Then the charge nurse decided he should come up and park himself on my bed, yanking the blanket off me, telling me to talk to him, to look at him. 'You can't avoid men all the time. You've got to start somewhere. And you've got to start speaking to me.' I became hysterical.

The day I ran away, everyone kept coming up to ask why I was lying on the bed. They told me to come down, to socialize and I did for a while. Downstairs were a couple of old women and men patients and the male nurses. I thought, 'I just can't cope with this. I shall never survive Christmas. I just have to get out.'

No one noticed me go. I didn't know where I was going, and it was lucky I had some money in my coat pocket. I started wandering along, and saw a bus so I got on it. When I got far enough away, dreading them coming after me any minute, I got on another bus to some town. There, I wandered around for hours, I didn't know where to go next. Everywhere there were Christmas carols playing, and, listening to them, I decided suddenly to go up and see the children.

Over the following four days I jumped on and off buses, remembering stops I'd seen when I'd last travelled up by train. In the Midlands I stayed in a hotel to avoid the men who came up to me in the street. By then I felt mentally and physically drained and so tired, but I was determined to see the children, and this kept me going, I suppose. I hadn't eaten. On the ward, I'd been surviving on a piece of toast a day. No one seemed to notice, and now I felt very ill. I stayed in the hotel a couple of days. The first morning, my face and hands were all red and swollen. I couldn't move out of bed. The maid kept coming to clean the room, but I told her to go away, to leave me alone. Why they let me stay I don't know. I must have looked an awful sight; I was getting up and sleeping in the same clothes, and not eating at all.

When I left the hotel, I continued north, arriving at the house of my ex-husband, who wasn't exactly pleased to see me. He'd heard I'd gone missing. The police were looking for me with tracker dogs. He brought the social worker and she told me I had to go back. 'But I've used all the money I had. I only came to see my children.

for Christmas.' She made out a travel warrant, and after a long train journey I went back to the hospital and a telling off.

I don't remember much more up to the time I was discharged, when I found myself on my home doorstep, thinking it's all going to start again.

Now I'm cleaning out my home, packing memories away in cartons and boxes, moving out and into a hostel which offers accommodation and counselling over a period of up to two years. I very much live from day to day, trying to cope, to get through the hours, the times I spend alone, wishing someone would come and talk to me, to listen and believe. Not one of the professional services has been near since I left hospital: my social worker, my doctor, and so on. It would be easy to give up. What is keeping me going now is the thought of starting afresh, a new life beginning in a new area where there might be the kind of help I need. I'm still punishing myself for the past, still cutting and scratching as a means of coping with the feelings I can't get to inside.

The social worker hasn't visited me here at home to see the way I'm living, and now she's on holiday there is no one to see me in her place. My doctor thinks I'm exaggerating, making up stories, and becoming hysterical. He'll only end up sending me back into the mental hospital, but that doesn't solve anything. It can only ever put off the real problem, the problem which is at the heart of all this.

The DHSS has paid me nothing for the two months I was in hospital. Sickness benefit has been disallowed because I don't have enough insurance contributions to cover it. Meanwhile, rent, gas, telephone, electric, are all mounting, and with an overdraft at the bank, everybody is asking for their share. The DHSS have now asked me to write another letter to them giving them, yet again, details of dates and times and payments, asking for medical certificates that were already sent while I was in hospital. We go over the same details time and time again — an ever-decreasing circle. I just can't cope with it all on my own.

I'm going out of my mind. I keep being sick. I'm still waiting for this place at the hostel to come up. Meanwhile, I'm trying to keep busy packing, living from one hour to the next. It's hard. I can't allow myself to feel, to be hurt. I feel so awfully alone.

The last time I visited Dee in her home she had totally given up.

She sat, mutilated, alone, afraid. Her bath was full of burn holes, and her face and arms were slashed with cuts from glass. She had lost her reason to live. No one seemed to want to know. No one seemed to care. I spent ages that day looking for something to give her strength and the courage to face her present and future in spite of her past.

One of Dee's paintings. Painting allowed her to cut beneath the abusiv feelings and find inner peace.

In the garage I found paintings she had done which had been broken for glass with which she used to cut and mutilate herself. On the walls were evidence of these same paintings, beautiful scenes depicting that inner peace she felt within if only she could cut deep enough, through those abusive feelings which were her legacy from the past.

I took some of the paintings with me, those still intact, reminding myself of her promise that if I could prove she had something to offer the world, something of herself, then she might at least have something to work with, to build on for the future. With the help of a sympathetic art gallery owner, we arranged an exhibition of Dee's paintings. With the money from sales, her survival became a reality. We could not take away her pain from the past, but we could show her how to make some good come out of all that bad.

Tina

My dad was sentenced by the courts to six years in prison for incest. When he found out that my family were going to be called as witnesses, he admitted that he had been having sex with both my older sister and myself.

When he had gone, Mum asked me to move back home. The social worker set up family therapy sessions with my dad, who was taken from the prison by a probation officer each time a session was to take place. For me the therapy didn't work; all the talking was done around me, and I just wasn't involved. I felt as if I didn't really belong there; I didn't have a voice. If the social worker wanted to ask a question, like asking my mum about whether or not she knew, she would say to the probation officer, 'Would you ask Mrs_____ if she knew her husband was having sex with her daughters?' Nothing was ever said directly to the person concerned and we just seemed to go round in circles. I felt completely out of things, and no one really asked how I felt in all of this. As far as they were concerned, Dad had been taken away, and my problem was solved.

Mum was drinking heavily. She still does. We rarely talk about what happened, and she still doesn't really know or understand. At home, the atmosphere is terrible. We kind of live with the problem and what happened to us without ever really dealing with it. We just don't know how, we haven't been shown. No one really talks without shouting and we argue all the time.

The only good thing to come out of all this is the relationship I now have with Dad. He's served three and a bit years of his sentence, and he's due for parole. He may be coming home this year to live, but what will happen then? Mum doesn't really want him here. My sisters don't want him, only I do. He's become my best friend. We haven't talked about what happened because Mum always there when we visit him in prison, together with a friend of his. I write to him once in a blue moon, so the real talking will have to come later. In the meantime, I enjoy the kind of relationship we have. That's the amazing thing I suppose, that despite everything which has happened, we have improved our relationship. We've learned to talk to one another. I'm looking forward to when he comes out.

Outside of the home, I'm a mess. I find myself going down to the health centre all the time, looking for someone to talk to, the right person to listen and understand. I can't talk about it; I find it easier to write but it still doesn't do anything for me. I haven't dealt with my problem as I know I should.

As far as relationships go, I can't make a go of them. I've just split up with my boyfriend because I can't handle the sex. Even some touching and other parts of togetherness feel wrong. And I know it goes back to what happened with my dad.

I've slept with my ex-boyfriend. The sex part was horrible, but the closeness was nice. I didn't get turned on and I didn't have an orgasm. I still remember that part with my dad. Maybe I'm being selfish, but I don't really know what to feel anymore; I don't know what is right and what is wrong.

Mary

Mary and John, now husband and wife, have known each other since they were youngsters. In fact, when Mary's father divorced her mother, John's mother became the new woman of the house.

Theirs is a story of conflict and confusion and divided loyalties because it involves both sets of parents, and two families which came under one roof. When Mary first began to acknowledge that her father had sexually abused her, both families attempted to deny what had happened, and viewed her with contempt and scorn, as an alien waging war on their home. No one in either family then or since has attempted to understand the aching sense of rejection and hurt which is the inheritance Mary's father has left her to cope with today.

Gradually, the past becomes an intrinsic part of the present, and Mary is plagued by pits of depression and self-doubts, particularly after the birth of her first child. She needs to know that their son at least will be protected from the same experience. She feels an over-riding sense of anger at what has been done to her in the past and a growing sense of outrage that he can actually have got away with it for so long.

On Tuesday 14 April 1987, Mary made an appointment with a solicitor to ask what could be done in the way of prosecuting her father. She wanted him to recognize incest as a crime. The solicitor was sympathetic enough to urge that she go for a public prosecution.

On Wednesday 22 April 1987, an appointment was made with a detective to put that prosecution in motion. A statement was taken from Mary covering her basic early experiences. The main problem at this stage was producing the kind of evidence admissible in court, the obvious difficulty being that it happened so long ago.

The effects are there. Mary is a product of her past and it will not let her go. It is she who is paying the price. Still there are the nightmares, pushing her through past experiences over and over again.

At this time there was also an increase in physical abuse in the form of beatings from her father. Once Mary had wanted to go home, back to her mother, but ended up having to go to hospital the next day with burst blood vessels in her hand. She had been using it to shield her head from her father's blows. That evidence, at least, is there in the hospital records.

Mary would fake her periods to get out of intercourse. She was kept out of school regularly as her school reports bear witness. Absenteeism rose from the few and infrequent two or three times per term when she was living with her mother, to as much as 40 days away, when her father could abuse her while her brother was out.

When Mary was 14, her father thought she might be pregnant, and she was made to insert an animal syringe and to wash herself out with washing-up liquid on a regular basis until her period began.

Her father tried very hard to convince Mary that they shared a very special kind of relationship which no other father and daughter had. He would make love to his girlfriend in his bed, and then once she had left, forced Mary to do the same. He started to see the woman he is with today when Mary was 16. When Carol moved into their family home the following year, the physical and sexual violence towards Mary stopped, but then the mental abuse began. Things finally came to a head when Carol threatened to leave if Mary did not go. Mary in turn became frightened that all the physical and sexual abuse would start again. At 19, she ran away from home.

A statement of what had taken place between Mary and her father was passed on to the police in the area where they had been living at the time. The statement described how:

- Oral sex was frequently forced upon her

- She was bathed, shaved and had olive oil massaged into her breasts. She also had to massage olive oil into her father. This ended up being a full body massage for her father, happening several times over their period together

● Sexual intercourse took place almost every night.

Four weeks later, Mary received a telephone call to say that they were going to question her father, following which she heard nothing. Later, she phoned the station to ask what had happened, and they said her father had admitted to certain parts of the statement. The case was with the district prosecutor, and the police assured Mary that there would certainly be a prosecution and that her father could go to prison for up to five years.

On 14 July 1987, the police again telephoned Mary to say that they would not now be prosecuting. A detective told Mary that her father was a broken man and had suffered greatly when he had to go to the police station for questioning. He was full of remorse and shame and seemed sorry for what he had done. It was implied that now that Mary had her own family, she ought to let things rest.

But Mary cannot let it rest, her memories of the past still haunt her, and she has suffered for too long. By bringing what happened into the open, she has now lost all family and friends, yet she herself has done no wrong. The man who should be punished still goes free without really realizing the crime he committed all those years ago, and for which his daughter still suffers today.

Mary is today currently involved in the mammoth task of collating evidence and statements from people she was in contact with in her past in the hope of bringing out that crime — statements such as from a teacher who taught during her time at school.

To whom it may concern

I knew Mary _____ for the five years she attended _____ and came into close contact with her during her last two years when I taught her RE and English. I was also her form teacher in the fourth year, and thus responsible for her pastoral care. It is probably true to say that I knew her better than anyone else at school, apart from her friend and classmate Susan.

She was a difficult pupil who seemed to find it hard to relate to her peers. She would complain that 'nobody liked her', but did not realize that she herself rebuffed all offers of friendship, and was aggressive in her attitude towards those she suspected — often wrongly — of patronizing her. Susan stood loyally by her in her frequent quarrels with other girls in the form and tried to show her that her own prickly attitude drove others away.

From the first, I was very concerned about Mary. I felt that there was a very unhappy person here. As I grew to know her better, and gained her trust, I began to recognize how much she had been hurt by the breakdown of her parents' marriage, and how deeply ambivalent were her feelings towards them both. Her natural affection for her mother was mixed with a deep anger at what she saw as the rejection of herself, her brother and her father. She was fiercely loyal to her father who had stayed to look after her and her brother. At the same time, she resented the burden placed on her in having to wash, cook and clean, and generally run the family home.

On one occasion, I arranged a residential weekend and at first Mary expressed an interest in the visit, while saying that she did not think her father would let her go. I pointed out how valuable the experience would be, and she said she would ask him. A couple of days later, she told me that she would not be coming, as her father had said he needed her at home. 'Surely he can manage without you for one weekend?' I said. 'You don't know him,' she said despondently, 'he never wants me to go anywhere.' And indeed, she did not join the group on this or the later visit we made.

As time went on, I became increasingly worried about Mary, who seemed to be continually exhausted and often tearful. Her concentration was poor, she missed odd days for no real reason (though always bringing a note of excuse from her father), and her homework was rarely, if ever, done. She finally confided to me one day that her father refused to allow her to do homework until all the other household tasks had been done, and even then, poured abuse on her for doing it at all, saying there was no point in it.

I suggested that I write to, or see, her father to explain the importance of her regular attendance and homework, and to try to get him to see that she could not be expected to cope with running a home without any help at her age. Her reaction was one of extreme agitation — almost of terror. She begged me not to contact her father.

'Please, please, Miss, please don't,' she said. 'He'd go mad if he thought I'd been moaning, if I was saying anything to anyone outside the family. He'd kill me if he thought I was talking to you like this.'

'That's all very well', I said, 'and I know it's difficult for him, but he can't use you as a substitute wife.'

When I said this, I was actually thinking of the house-keeping aspect, but something in Mary's reaction, something in her eyes, made me suddenly wonder if there could be more in what I had said than I had intended. She did not reply, except to repeat, 'Please ... please ... don't say anything.'

I decided, though not without trepidation, to risk a direct question.

'Mary, has your father ever interfered with you?'

She was distraught. 'No... no... no...' she insisted. 'Please miss, don't...'

'Are you sure?' I said. 'Because if there is anything like that that you are not happy about, we *can* help. Something can be done, you know.'

Again, she cried out 'No... no... I'm all right, there's nothing like that.'

But her eyes belied her words, and I had a strong feeling that her friend Susan, who was present, was of my opinion. We both tried to persuade Mary that if incest had been happening she must tell us so that something could be done about it. But she became more and more distressed, begging us to stop talking about it, and saying repeatedly 'No, no, you mustn't say anything to anybody. I'll kill myself if you do.' Then she collapsed into sobs again.

In the face of her insistent denials, and of her obvious fear of her father's anger, I was at a loss to know what to do. I had heard that her father had been very aggressive and unpleasant to another member of staff who had visited him about Mary during the third year, and that he had a violent temper. (Mary and Susan had told me of an occasion when he had found them looking at a pop magazine bearing a picture of a black singer, and had ripped it up, while abusing the singer and the girls for looking at it.)

The climate of opinion was very different ten years ago.

The general public knew little about child abuse; it was considered rare, and a common attitude was that only the prurient would suspect it. I feared that if I acted on my suspicions, not only would I lose Mary's confidence altogether, but I might be faced with an action for slander or defamation. I had no proof, no real evidence, only a very strong feeling that Mary was lying to me.

I had often spoken to my husband of my concern for Mary, and that night I told him of the incident, saying, 'I just felt like bringing her back here, putting her to bed and pampering her a bit. What she needs is some love and attention, and to get away from that father of hers.' My husband felt that there was nothing I could do, except what I was already doing — giving Mary my friendship, and the knowledge that she could talk to me when she needed to.

Neither Mary nor I referred to that conversation again while she was at school. I tried to help her as much as I could with her schoolwork, and frequently comforted her when she was upset and tired, as she so often was. She was in no state to undertake public examinations, and there is no doubt in my mind that she was prevented from achieving her academic potential and was deeply hurt psychologically by her father's attitude and behaviour.

I saw her at a school reunion some months after she left school, and she told me she was leaving home, which I thought the best possible thing for her. We exchanged Christmas greetings for some years, and she let me know of her engagement. I often thought of her and hoped she had found happiness.

Since Mary telephoned and asked me to make this statement, I have bitterly regretted not trusting my intuition eight years ago. I knew in my heart that her denial was a lie, and yet I did nothing. I find it hard to forgive myself.

Head of Language Faculty

Mary's task of gathering evidence continues, and she hopes to prosecute her father in the future.

Sue

I live as a 'lady of the night', a prostitute. It's a living, not one I would have chosen for myself, but at least one in which I can stay alive and remain in control. I can call 'time'. I can use what my father taught me, and in this, he gave me a good education!

It's easy for people to judge me for what they see I am when they don't know what my life was like before. Maybe they would be in the same position given my set of circumstances. I know many of my friends were abused as children. Looking back, I still don't see that any of us could have had any other choice.

My dad used me. He took his pleasure. He was in control, and he could do so because I was a minor. He was the adult, and I was the child. It was his word against mine; I just didn't have a chance. What else could I do except run away when the authorities kept taking me back into the danger, instead of away from it? Home was where the hurt was. I had to live with that every single day of my life after I started my periods. To my dad, I was a woman. We were having an affair. The beginning of my periods marked a new era, a new kind of relationship, the same but different, and I was there for him. That was the way he looked at things. That was the way it was.

Even when my dad was not touching me, he was there, watching me, undressing me with his eyes. The pressure would build in both of us, mine out of fear, his out of lust. Then in the evening he would be inside my bedroom, inside my bed, inside me.

It sounds dirty, and it was dirty; it made me feel unclean. My mother knew what was happening, but she couldn't seem to find a way out. It maybe kept him away from her.

There came a point when I could go home for something to eat when I was on the run, and she would feed me and I could get a few hours sleep. But when Dad returned home, I would sneak out of the back door as he came in the front.

When finally I stayed away I lived in squats, anywhere where there was room. There was usually a corner of a floorboarded room to be found where I could spend the night, especially when it was cold outside. I earned enough to buy food, living any way I could. I soon learned how. Men would pay me for the kind of things I'd done with my dad and it was a way to stay alive. When I passed my eighteenth birthday, I wasn't a minor any more. When the police found me, they didn't have to take me home.

When I was 16, I found out I was pregnant. Life wasn't easy; I had a child to support, but still I couldn't see any other way out. By this time, living as I was had more or less become a way of life; it was what I knew. Most of all, it kept me safe, it gave me somewhere to belong.

My friends and I grouped together, helping one another. We were all in the same boat. Society saw us as outcasts, except those who wanted to use what we had to offer, and pay for the privilege, so we needed each other in order to survive.

Today, I know I'm lucky to be alive. I live one day at a time. It's the most that I can do. Some days are good, some days are bad, but at least I can stay in control.

Jane

I went to see my doctor the other day. It has taken years to bring myself to this, and the smear test I had was abnormal. At the moment, I am in a lot of pain. I have just had my first period for two years. Now the pain is almost unbearable. I have decided not to get treatment if there is anything wrong. I can't live with myself any more anyway. My family have told me for years I don't deserve to live, so this will be it, the end. No one will have to bother about me then any more.

My dad says I'm not capable of love, but then I've been taught to hate. What is it about me anyway that makes them do this to me, to cause me so much pain? Maybe I deserve it. Maybe I was born for this, and this is my purpose in life. Oh, I do feel unhappy. I see all this pain in the world, and those poor children on television hurt by adults they trust and love, like me. I would love to offer one of them a home. I don't think I will ever be able to bear my own child.

I feel very vicious towards myself. Sometimes I burn myself a lot and my husband won't let me have a carving knife for fear of what I will do. I don't have enough courage to kill myself, but I can at least hurt myself. It is the kind of punishment I've been trained to do.

Why am I so terrible? Is it true you can be born bad? I feel so sick when I look in the mirror. It's not the outside, it's what's inside that is so bad. I'm bad at the core and that cannot be put right.

A few days ago, I decided to try again to kill myself. I just couldn't live with this pain of being me any more. It hurts so much. And it is always there, a part of me. There in the morning. There at night. There to haunt me in my dreams. There is no escape from it.

I said goodbye to my husband, and I phoned the doctor, I don't know why. I made an appointment to tell him I wouldn't be seeing him any more. I spoke to him, thanking him for his help. He asked me to come to see him with my husband, so I did. He just couldn't understand what it was I was trying to say to him through all the emotion, all he could see were the physical signs of trauma.

He ended the visit by saying that he had done all he could and felt he had failed as far as I was concerned. He would set up a meeting with a psychiatrist and see how it went from there. Otherwise there were always the pills, but then he couldn't even give me those for fear that I might take the lot.

The visit to the psychiatrist was awful. He didn't want to hear anything I tried to say, he made comments about the amount my GP had written in note form about me. He said that I must have sex, and that I could if I really wanted, there was nothing physically preventing a union between my husband and myself. Children of five and under rarely have memories he said, and I had only imagined things which I thought had happened before the age of six. If I changed my outward appearance I would begin to like myself better. Everything would then come right.

My visit to the psychiatrist lasted 20 minutes. In that time I must have said less than ten words. He made me feel he had already decided what was wrong with me before I stepped through his door, and he was trying to put me into a slot which I didn't fit because I didn't belong. Fitting me in would make it easier for him, that way he could more quickly deal with my symptoms.

What the psychiatrist probably didn't notice was that prior to the appointment I had a perm. I bought myself new clothes. I was trying to change my image, to give myself a new face, and make myself into the kind of person that I could maybe live with better, to be happier with myself. But changing my outward appearance apparently didn't alter me inside. It didn't work out the way he said it would.

I felt like dirt, inadequate and confused as I made my way home. I became so hysterical that my husband couldn't cope, he just didn't know what to do for the best. Those we would normally have gone to for help had let us down. So who was there to listen? Who was there to care?

My doctor wanted to hear about the visit. The psychiatrist had been in touch and diagnosed that I was an 'attention-seeking female', so I decided not to go back. They couldn't help, they couldn't understand. The doctor wants me to go back, to see the psychiatrist again and go on a repeat prescription of Valium to calm me down. If I don't go, the doctor sees it as a rejection of help, and an unwillingness to help myself.

So now I feel more trapped than ever. I have it on good authority that all I am doing is attention seeking. Am I? Is that what the pain of these memories is? Is that what I'm all about?

Even now, I remember how I was told from an early age that plain girls had to take what was on offer and not be choosey. Everything was done for my own good. I shouldn't question. I shouldn't resist. As soon as I stopped being fed by my family, I was expected to do everything for myself, whether I was capable or not: feeding myself, washing myself, putting on my clothes and shoes, combing hair, using cutlery, etc. Actually, a neighbour taught me a lot. I had to go out after I got up, without breakfast, and then stay out till bed. I used to get food from that neighbour, or go to an evening group held at a nearby school for poor people where I got a currant bun and a cup of orange. Sunday was murder because dad would be home. I went to Sunday school, and returned to a beating and a bath. I used to associate Sundays with hurt and confusion and dread. I still do. I still get that awful churning feeling inside. . .

When I was about eight I used to wear as many pairs of pants as I could to keep him out. I tried to stay away from the house as much as possible, but then I was kept off school on his two afternoons home from work. I remember once my mother was out shopping and the truant officer asked her where I was. Innocently she said I should be at school, but all the time she knew where I was, and what was being done to me. He paid her money for it. Do mothers always sell their children? I have nothing else to compare it with, because this became my normal everyday life, something I had to accept.

When a psychiatrist tells me I imagine it, it makes me frightened that I might be going mad. To know and to feel something which I can only imagine must mean I am mad. Mustn't it? What other explanation can there be?

Understanding the problem

Everyone has bad experiences. Some of us have more memorable and traumatic ones than others. It is these experiences which
make us into the kind of people we are today. Good or bad, they
become our learning pattern for what is to come. When our
experiences are disturbing and horrifying, stronger than real life,
richer than fiction, as many in this book will appear to the non-
believer, it places an additional burden on the survivor. Not only
will they have to learn to accept themselves in the light of their
experiences and cope in the aftermath of abuse, but they will also
have the stigma of outsiders' judgement and disbelief.

Some experiences, such as those contained in this book, you
may find difficulty in relating to, and it is easy to judge when you
have perhaps not shared the same early learning pattern. It isn't
easy to comprehend another's life when it is so vastly different
from our own. We reach the limit of our understanding. Our own
lifestyle and early learning experiences are what we know best;
they are our norm. We can accept that without question. But no
two people are the same and just because another's normality is
different doesn't mean it has to be wrong, or that we should judge
that person because of it. We will have had a different beginning,
creating different values for us, different ways of coping and absorb-
ing the truth about ourselves. We therefore relate only in part
to another's emotion, and perhaps not at all to the reality of their
situation. We may not comprehend at all how experience con-
trols what happens to that person for the rest of their lives.

That is why it is important for survivors like Dee, Tina, Mary,
Sue and Jane to share their experiences, to be as graphic and as
detailed as possible. The sharing helps to put their lives in perspective, and to accept the people they are now because of that
past. It also enables the reader to identify with their feelings as

a whole, to acknowledge the outcome, and to feel the pain, the humiliation, the shame, the guilt, the suffering which is the burden they carry today.

The first thing that becomes apparent in reading the shared experiences is the amazing similarity between the survivors portrayed. At times they could all be the same woman, yet neither one has spoken to the other. They have all written out their lives independently of the rest.

Surely this means that, rather than individuals suffering in isolation, they have a collective problem. No matter who the abuser was, whether grandfather, grandmother, father, mother, brother, sister, uncle, aunt, babysitter, teacher or friend, the emotions which are left are the same.

In the beginning, through no fault of their own, each survivor took on board an early learning experience handed down by adults who betrayed their trust. In many cases, where survivors are able to talk out their feelings and work through family therapy, it is possible to trace abuse back over many generations. Thus, the grandfather was abused by his own father, and he by his father before; the mother was abused by her father and he by his father before, and so on. No one can say how far back we would have to go to trace our source of abuse today. That fact alone implies that sexual abuse is not a new thing brought on by a permissive and violent society, but rather that it is only now coming to the fore because people are more willing to listen and to believe. The victims are at last being given a voice.

For the survivors, the abuse which first took place in childhood dictates that in later life they will feel inferior, used and abused, with an overwhelming loss of self-worth. They will be looking for the kind of love which perhaps doesn't really exist at all. They are reaching out for a dream, while at the same time running away from a past that will not let them go. For some, every waking and sleeping moment is a nightmare. Everyday routines trigger off a moment of memory, and they are left in a no-man's land between then and now. Inside, they feel lost, hurt, lonely, sad, confused, afraid. Like Peter Pan children who have never grown up, they have not been given the chance of the kind of love which enables them to grow and to move on into the future. Inside each and every survivor of abuse there is still that child which needs to be liked, which is reaching out for someone who will not betray their trust.

At some point in her early life each woman studied in this book was controlled by an abuser. Being controlled means that, even when the abuser is gone, his teaching remains, undermining her confidence, dictating how her life will be led in the future. Unless they are given the chance to re-educate themselves, this can become the learning pattern for life, setting a precedent for what is to come, for survivors of abuse, their children, and for future generations.

Even more surprising, perhaps, is the fact that, however degrading and painful the abuse suffered as a child, and however much victims may recognize the need to get away from it, their lives seem to be (to the outsider) dedicated in its pursuit. Even in their first relationships, victims are attracted to people who appear to everyone else but them to be carbon copies of their first abuser. It seems to outsiders that they are actively seeking further abuse, but all they are looking for is their own peace of mind. They are searching for that special someone who is there for them and who they can trust — someone who will not betray them, and in whom they can believe.

Through the experiences of Dee, Tina, Mary, Sue and Jane, we are able to empathize and to see that all were abused at first by someone within the home, someone who they should have been able to trust. All had that trust betrayed. Just like myself and many thousands of others, they then embarked on a search, a search for someone to trust, someone to understand, someone to believe. It is during that search that we allow ourselves to get into very dangerous situations. In our subconscious there is the hope that they will say 'I don't want anything from you. It's okay by me. I will understand.' We need that special someone who will make no demands on us, someone who will believe and not judge. It seems that those people are few and far between when you need them.

The arrival of the professionals seems to exacerbate the problem. There are no experts on sexual abuse, and understanding can only ever come about when survivors feel comfortable and safe and trusting enough to share their experiences, their fears, their own needs of self. Professionals vary, as does the help, from one area to another. Some are more willing to learn from the sufferer, others are not; the latter placing themselves on a pedestal alongside the knowledge they have gained through academic study and statistical reports. They close their minds to what the survivor is trying to say, and hear only the symptoms, as they analyse and offer appropriate treatment and pill remedies according to what they have been taught. There is no cure as such for sexual abuse, but there are means of coping with its effects. Different things work for different people, and sadly, it seems that the kind of caring professional who is willing to work with the abused to try to find what works best for them is scarce.

Many of the shared experiences which have gone before followed a very familiar pattern; psychiatrists who pumped the victims full of drugs; doctors who told them to pull themselves together; counsellors who could not and should not counsel in this field; family members who ignored the problem because they could not cope and were afraid to deal with it. Most of these people acted on the premise, 'I do not understand it, therefore it does not exist.'

How can anyone help if they refuse to even begin to understand why the abused feel so dirty, guilty, evil, unclean, and responsible for what has and is happening to them? Experiences such as those related by the survivors in this book are sadly all too common. For every one of these experiences there are hundreds more following the same pattern of abuse. But there is hope, there are those who found peace, and if they did, all victims of abuse can. It does mean sharing experiences, learning to face fears and those things which make the victim feel bad, finding out what feels right for them, looking for the kind of person they can trust, who will work alongside them to reach a better understanding of the whole. It means helping the abused to move on, and allowing them to place the guilt and the shame firmly back with their abuser, where it belongs.

PART THREE
The abuser

A circle of abuse

People who perpetrate sexual abuse, whether on children or adults, are not green-eyed, horned monsters. They look like ordinary, everyday people like you and me. There is nothing on the outside to tell you they are any different; they don't look as if they would be a risk. Many are so mild in their manner that they just don't seem capable of abuse. Many are attractive to the opposite sex. And they come from all walks of life. In meeting them for the first time you probably wouldn't even know they were different. But what is probably more important, neither would they.

Okay, so maybe they act weird once in a while. Maybe they can even justify their actions. 'She or he asked for it.' 'She or he needed to be punished.' 'She or he was my enemy, invading my space.' 'She or he knew what was coming, and said yes.' 'She or he consented, I wasn't doing anything wrong.' Just because they live in a different normality from us doesn't mean they don't mean what they say. Very often they believe they are telling the truth. But it is the truth as they see it, because it is a part of what they have lived with all their lives, and they can't see they are doing anything wrong.

Abusers usually have to reach a crisis in their life before they begin to realize they have a problem they need to resolve. (See Fig 1) Very often, the first few times it happens they ignore it, hoping it will go away. Then comes the moment when they catch a glimmer of the truth, or are confronted with someone else's normality which doesn't quite fit their own. They reach that moment of conflict and they know they will have to go for outside help. But who can they talk to? Where can they go? There seem more places to help those who have been hurt than places for those causing the pain.

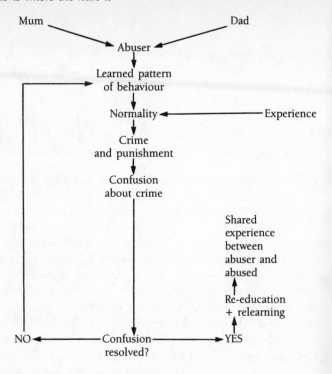

Fig. 1

Then they really begin to get worried about what is happening to them in their life, because the answer suddenly doesn't seem that straightforward. It isn't like going to the doctor for an ailment and getting a pill to make it all better. They start asking themselves questions, 'Is it the other person's fault, just as I first thought? Or is it something else, something within my own make-up?' The possibility is frightening, and they get scared about who they really are. How can they find out the truth?

When they look at the lists of agencies available, offering counselling and help, nothing immediately seems to apply to them. It is always difficult when they don't know the exact nature of the problem anyway. There are those who approach their doctor, hoping for that pill to make it all come right. Maybe their doctor gives them pills on repeat prescription, to help them sleep, to calm them down, to stop the now increasing panic attacks and depression they are feeling as a result of the unresolved problem inside. But it is still there, a part of them, a part of the conflict which becomes a part of their life.

So for a while they go round in circles, tracing and retracing their steps, until finally they find themselves being challenged as they are charged and sentenced to a term of imprisonment for something called rape or sexual abuse or incest, which they don't even understand.

I have met such men both in and out of prison. Many of them are not so much bad as sad, having spent years looking for something which nobody else even knows is there. I am trying to help such men understand the nature of their crime, to tell them what the rape and incest and sexual abuse is really all about. Together we share experiences, abuser and abused. I am someone who is there for them to talk to. But my presence does not condone what they have done. I cannot lighten their sentence or offer them the forgiveness they need. In the end, they have to learn to live with themselves. Only they can bring about change by wanting to stop the same thing happening again. Different things work for different people, and we have to find what works best for them.

I see my role initially as one of sharing, using my own abuse to help them understand what it means to be sexually abused, to realize the kind of hurt they have caused. And then, moving on from there, we begin to work back over their past, from their first memory as a child. It takes a special kind of strength to go back and recall mistakes, confronting fear, admitting abuse. Together we remember what they have done, and hurts done to them which have remained unresolved, misunderstood, the kind of pain which, added to their general pattern of life, goes towards making them into the kind of people they are today. As long as they are open and honest with me, I will work with them; I will be there for them. Only when we have collated every bit of information possible about their past, often with the valuable help of family, friends, victims, and all those willing and able to take part, only then can we make a start on relearning and re-educating for the future.

When we meet for the first time it is important that they remember their reactions, what they say, where they look, how they feel, what they think, and afterwards that they write down everything they can remember about the meeting. To begin with they are often suspicious, looking for motives, a reason why I might be willing to share and to talk. They need to know I am a safe person to confide in, because they are going to discuss their most secret fears and frustrations with me, when they have never fully trusted anyone before. There is a testing period, a time of getting to know each other, when we state our boundaries, and begin a friendship on which to build.

Whether we meet in a prison visiting room, a special visits room, in a room offered by an outside agency, or in their own home, it is important to identify those first vital feelings.

Often we role-play, pretending we are in a cafe and that I am choosing a table at which to sit. Very often they respond by believing I choose that place for a purpose, perhaps because I am attracted to them, and by sitting with them I am agreeing to more. I am blonde, and this fact alone seems to incite, fostering the belief that I am looking for a good time. It is also the kind of myth fostered by the media, using stars like Marilyn Monroe, Jayne Mansfield and Brigitte Bardot. We discuss options: what if I were short or long-haired, had dark or red hair, was slim, medium, or large build? While pornographic magazines and films show models who are seen to be enjoying acts of obscenity and illegal sex, men who are considered at risk of committing abuse can take that into real life situations of rape and sexual abuse and think it's okay.

Still in a role-play situation, they share what they would be most likely to do next if there was really someone like me sitting at their table. One man said he would wait until I stood up to leave, and then would follow me with a knife, waiting behind a bush for the opportune moment to strike and to rape. Another would try making conversation, and when this failed, would find out where I lived, again following me until the time seemed right. Someone else would have spoken to several ladies before me, and when I too denied him, he would feel let down, alienated, depressed and rejected to the point that I became the one who had to be for him.

I would not attempt to offer any form of rational explanation for an abuser's behaviour. Nor do I consider myself qualified to offer therapy that is guaranteed to work in the future for men who have sexually abused. My main function is to help them to understand what they have done and the hurt they have inflicted on another, whether on an outsider or on one of his own family

I offer them a voice, for I believe that it is only by listening with an open mind to their side as well as to the abused that we are ever going to be able to understand the problems of sexual abuse to find the kind of answers we need. Helping the abused to escape is dealing with one side of the problem in isolation. It isn't getting to the source. And while the abuser is left to take his learned pattern of behaviour elsewhere, someone else in the future is going to be hurt and destroyed.

As I have said, I cannot take away an abuser's past, nor can I condone his crime, but through sharing experiences, abuser with abused, talking out all the hurt, the shame, the guilt, I can at least help him to realize what it means to rape and sexually abuse. If someone does not do this, he is left with words which he does not understand, words like rape, incest and sexual abuse. Abusers cannot understand or reform when they have no way of knowing about the feelings which go alongside the words. In their ignorance, they continue to protest their innocence, while the media builds them into all kinds of monsters of evil, lobbying for them to be locked away where they can no longer do harm. But what then? What happens on their moment of release? They cannot stay incarcerated for ever, and it still isn't dealing with the problem at source.

Prison, which becomes an abuser's ultimate home, cannot change an offender without therapy running alongside. And many prisons still have no therapy to offer. Without it, an abuser cannot be helped. He has no way for change to take place, and no reason to help himself. He remains the same kind of man he was, and over the period of his sentence he will become more and more angry at what society is doing to him. He will be incensed with feelings of being victimized, persecuted and gaoled for something he feels he didn't do.

Sharing experiences between abused and abuser works. At least it gives the abuser the chance to understand his crime, giving him something for the future, and the incentive to change the kind of person he has become. Otherwise, for many it is already too late.

Gus's experience

Currently serving an 18 months' prison sentence for indecent assaults on boys

I was one of a family of four. There are my parents, my sister and myself.

Since I was a child it seems I was a victim. I was born with an ear and speech impediment, and between the ages of 4 and 14 I was back and forth to the hospital for operations. I have had a total of 16 operations. There were long periods when I was away from school, which interrupted my general education. The children at school used to be very cruel and called me names.

I was seven years old when my parents began to seek divorce. My mother tried to take her life. It was at this same time that my first experience of sexual abuse occured.

My parents had already separated. My sister at that time was 12. We had a babysitter, a woman in her twenties. I remember her as being of normal height and build and with blonde hair.

When she came to the house she would sometimes tie my sister to the radiator and then take me into the bedroom. She would strip me and then she would play with my private parts and kiss me all over. When she was at our house this would happen perhaps twice during an evening over a period of three to four months. I did not want her to do it and I was very scared. I didn't tell anyone about this until I was 26 when I told my probation officer. I kept it to myself because I felt very dirty and ashamed about what had happened. My sister told mother about being tied to the radiator, and the babysitter stopped coming, but I don't think that the matter was reported to the police.

When I was ten years old, I was in a house fire. It was Christmas Day, 1970. The fire caused a lot of damage but no one was seriously hurt. I was missing my father a lot and I remember wishing he was home with us. By this time I was in a special school because educationally I was falling behind the rest of the children.

The second incident of sexual abuse that I experienced happened when I was 13, in 1974. It involved a local man who was a bus driver.

One day when I was coming home from school, he asked me to go out for a drive and I accepted. He took me out of the town and parked the car. We walked along a riverbank by some trees. There was no one around. He took down his trousers and pants and asked me to play with him. I refused and he forced me down to the ground. He tried to take off my trousers and pants and I was struggling to get away. He managed to get them down and then he buggered me. I can remember it being very painful.

I did manage to get away, but he chased me and caught me and then physically beat me. He got me back into the car and then dropped me off in town. I was so shocked that I couldn't exactly remember what had happened. Again, I didn't tell anyone about this until 1987, basically because I was very scared of him. It was bad enough having to see him around without causing any further hassle.

I now feel angry and bitter that I was taken advantage of in this way. I was having learning difficulties at the time and visiting hospital with my hearing problem. Both these incidents of abuse only added to my problems.

I left school at 16 and have committed several indecent assaults on boys since I was 17 years old. My last offence of gross indecency consisted of me touching a boy's bare bottom. The boy was nine years old. The other offences are of a similar nature. The feelings I get when I commit these offences are similar to those I had when I myself was being abused.

In 1985, I started going to a basic education unit to improve myself, hoping to move on to a better standard of life. I also did life saving and first aid exams, both of which I passed. Then, in 1987, I became a member of a church, and by proclaiming myself a Christian, I had hopes of enjoying a new life with other people there. But today, I am serving a prison sentence. I do not seem to be able to stop committing sexual offences against boys.

Jerry's experience

Currently serving a life sentence with a recommendation to serve 15 years as a Category A prisoner in a maximum security prison. He was found guilty of rape, attempted rape, robbery and murder.

I'm out walking. It's not late, about 7.00pm, and I'm walking down a shortcut. It's pretty cold and there's snow on the ground. I see a woman walking down the shortcut and I don't think she's seen me. When she passes, I hit her from behind, knocking her to the floor, and punch her hard. I am frightened, but the adrenalin is pumping so I get her to walk into a field. But she won't walk where I want because she is worried that I will chuck her into the big drain. Finally, I get her to walk a different way. I force her to strip and I rape her.

The attack lasts perhaps half an hour. At that time, I never consider how much it might affect her. After the initial attack, I don't have to use force, and as such it does not constitute violence in my eyes. I never think about the cold, or how it affects her mentally.

I am walking late at night when I come across a young woman. I pull her into a school playing field where I rape her. There is no violence at all, I never hit her. The act itself wasn't entirely one-sided, although by that I am not trying in any way to justify my actions or to say that she either deserved or enjoyed it. There is no doubt that it was against her will.

It's about 11.00pm. I have just walked my girlfriend home as I usually do. I'm going for a walk. I enjoy the night, not necessarily because of its obvious help for me to commit my crimes, but because it has more atmosphere and enables me to daydream.

It is after midnight when I catch a glimpse of someone crossing my path about a hundred yards ahead. I am at one corne

of a school and by cutting across diagonally, I manage to inter-
cept her in the school. I force her to walk towards a nursery, still
within the school, but before we get there, some dogs start bark-
ing. In response, I walk her to a prefab where I tell her to take
her jeans down, which she does, but she tells me she is having
a period. I take it no further.

For some reason, I move her on again, this time to a field just
through the school where I force her to have oral sex. However
I'm not really getting anything out of it so I stop her. I take her
purse. She has £25.30 from which I take £20.25, and I also take
something with her name on.

Shortly after first confronting her, I dropped a knife case. I try
to find it, but failing to do so, return home. In fact, later I found
it was only a few yards away.

I'm walking down a lane, just off the main estate. There's bushes
alongside both sides and so it's pretty secluded. It leads to a rub-
bish tip and there are also a couple of farmhouses along the lane.
I pass this woman. She's walking towards the estate and I'm walking
away from it. I don't remember talking to her or even anything
much about her, but I turn into the field and follow her.

About a hundred yards from the estate, I jump out of the bushes
and drag her into the ditch. I think my reason was to rob her,
but I panic. I remember thinking 'Who will be one of the first
people questioned about an attack on a woman?'

I start to stab her, and once I've started, I can't stop. I remember
thinking, 'God! She must be in pain.' I want to stop. I can't believe
what I've done. But I still search her bag and steal her purse.

Instead of running directly to my home, I run into the fields
and ditch the knife in a smallish drain. A little bit further, I ditch
the purse, minus the money, I then go home. My mother is at work,
but my sister who is 12 is home with a friend. I go to the sink
and wash my hands, then try to find some clothes.

My sister wants to go out and she's worried about locking up.
I tell her it will be all right and that I want to have a bath, which
I do. After I have changed clothes, I catch a bus and spend the
afternoon in a betting shop losing the money I stole. Then I meet
my girlfriend, by which time the news is out about the murder.

I react as if I know nothing. I don't want to think about it. That's
my way of living with what I've done. However, later in bed, I admit
it to my girlfriend. She gets up to go to work as normal, but I

get up with her and she decides instead to stay away from work. I go with her to her mother's where the police come to see me. I tell them, and they go to my home to check my story. There I am arrested.

I was born in 1962 and since 1982, I've been in prison. I've always been in trouble of one sort or another. I would steal anything and if caught, lie outright that I hadn't done anything wrong. It wasn't me! I played truant from every school I ever attended, but I was never illiterate. A bad speller, yes. Thick, no.

When we moved from our old neighbourhood onto the new sprawling estate, things went downhill. It was a kid's paradise, building sites, open fields, and a refuse tip. When I was about ten, I started to camp out in a nearby field overnight. This directly led me to a systematic robbing spree of parked cars for which I've never been charged. As you might guess, for a boy of ten it was a great game, it was Christmas every night! I used to approach every car as though it was a great lucky bag just waiting to divulge its hidden surprises. Me and my pals had hundreds of music cassettes, radios, tools and torches. My God, did we have torches!

Like all things, it progressed, and soon I was stealing from shops, and then breaking into houses. I was no stranger to the police. My first real contact with them was for shoplifting. It never worried me being in a police cell unfortunately, and I went through a series of appearances before the juvenile courts for such petty things as dumping litter, walking on a motorway, and armed trespass — which sounds serious, until you know that I was in a field with an air rifle.

When I was 16, I left school with no qualifications because I never bothered to take the final exams. I eventually got a job on a Youth Training Scheme with a caravan building firm. It was slave labour at £20 per week compared with the £16 a week I was getting on the dole. Everyone there seemed to be stealing items and I would nick all sorts of things, more often than not stuff I never needed. One day, it all came to a head when I hadn't bothered to go to work. My mother's friend went shopping with my mother, I broke into her house and stole the TV meter. I ended up getting caught for this and in turn admitted to a few other burglaries. The result was a sentence to Borstal training.

I did 34 weeks and, after the initial shock of prison, enjoyed it. I was released, but almost at once ended up doing a recall for another burglary. I did another 16 weeks and the only other appearance I had in court was for Actual Bodily Harm on my girl-friend's ex-boyfriend. Then I got into trouble over the rapes and murder.

I guess some people might wonder about parental guidance or the lack of it. I was never smothered in love by my family, but I wouldn't say they weren't a loving one. In their own way, they loved me, I'm sure, but that's said with hindsight and at the time it felt different.

My father was a long-distance lorry driver, then later he became a seaman, which meant he was often away from home. My mother was responsible for bringing me up and obviously punishing me when I was bad. As you might imagine, this was quite often. I remember getting some good hidings, but when I got bigger, there was little she could do. I have always been one for making my own deci-sions and accepting the consequences if I made the wrong ones. So nothing my parents said or did stopped me going my own way.

I am serving a life sentence for murder. I am also doing two ten-year sentences for rape, one six-year sentence for attempted rape, and five years for robbery. How that came about is not easy to explain, but I guess it goes back to one night when I was woken by my parents arguing. During the course of their fight, I learned that I wasn't the son of my father. My mother had been attacked and raped when she was about 16 and I was born as a result. I don't really know how it affected me, but I never let on the next day that I had heard anything.

The night I attacked and raped my first victim it was the first time I had gone all the way and had sex. I had had girlfriends, sure, and we had indulged in serious petting. But this was the first time for me for real. The actual sex act wasn't violent, which sounds stupid because of course it was, I just don't know how to explain it. Perhaps if I say it wasn't sadistic, it still isn't exactly it, but it's the best I can do.

The second attack took place in the following year. The rape lasted no more than ten minutes and there was no violence at all. She was obviously frightened — who wouldn't be? — but I honestly believe she got over it without much difficulty. It's hard for me to think anything bad about any of my victims, because in the end, that's what they all were — victims. However, to be fair to myself, I think it's all right to point out that some people are more casual in their attitude towards sex.

I don't think that my heart was really in the attack which happened after walking my girlfriend home. That might raise a few hackles, but I had the time to rape this woman, and I didn't. That's my view and other people involved might not agree. I was supposed to live at home and be on a curfew, but that never happened and I ended up living with my girlfriend's sister. Why my girlfriend stuck by me I don't know. Perhaps she really did love me after all, or perhaps it was just her show of loyalty.

Things weren't easy. I never saw my friends and I knew everyone was talking about me, but it didn't stop me going out. It's almost as if I was daring people to say something. I had taken to carrying a knife just in case someone did want trouble, but no one did.

The day I was out walking in the fields near the estate, I had nowhere else to go. As usual, I was skint. When I saw the woman walking down a secluded lane, without really thinking, I decided to steal her bag. When I took it I thought almost at once, 'Now you've done it!' and I panicked. I just reached instinctively for the knife and stabbed her again and again. Robbery was the motive, but I think there was also the dam breaking, releasing all my anger and frustration, all focused on destroying this woman, not because she was a woman, but because she was in the wrong place at the wrong time. The walking bomb that was me went off.

That was six years ago and the guilt will be with me forever. I don't believe in God. Where there is good and evil I can only hope that I am given the chance to do some good. I can never counter the evil I've done but I can die trying.

I can imagine people saying, 'I could never do that.' Don't believe it. I attacked the women thinking I wasn't doing them any permanent harm as very little force was used in the physical sense. What never entered my head was that these women couldn't just walk away like I could, they would always remember and they might not be able to cope. Some people who are raped never have a happy sex life again, not even with the partners they love. Some spend every day expecting it to happen again. The problem is not the physical, bad as that it is, but the mental pressure this puts them under. That is why people should learn that this is as disruptive as any other crime, if not more so, and should be treated as such.

Jerry's mother

I was raped by my mum's boyfriend, but I don't remember much about it. I was 17 years old, and not very wise. I was six months pregnant before I knew anything about it. I knew nothing about life and didn't understand what was happening to me at that time.

I went through a bad patch with my mother then, as she thought it should have been her child when she found I was pregnant by her boyfriend. She gave me a good hiding all the way from the doctor's to our house.

When Jerry was born he had yellow jaundice and I was accused of having a foreign baby. All things considered, it wasn't a very good beginning for him. I came out of hospital to another good hiding and name calling and my mum saying it was her son and not mine.

I'd met my husband while carrying Jerry, and told him about my being pregnant, which he seemed to understand. I loved him, so after Jerry was born, I moved in with Jim, trying to get away from my mother who sent police and social workers to try to make me go back home. I wasn't 18 until the October and I thought then that I could handle anything. Besides, anything was better than the situation at home.

Jerry was in contact with violence from the day he was born. I jumped from the frying pan into the fire. Jim was a married man with a family I didn't know about, and everything just got on top of me. I used to get depressed a lot of the time, and before I knew it, I was pregnant again.

Jerry would have been a year old when I lost my next baby. There was only Jerry and myself in the toilet and he had to go and kick on one of the other flats to get some help for me. I was eight months pregnant. When I lost the baby I developed milk fever and I was sent home from the hospital to my mother who, by then, had taken Jerry. She made my life hell, saying it was God's punishment for taking Jerry away from her.

I moved back in with Jim, but he spent a lot of time going out on his own. It caused arguments and many a good hiding for me, but I don't remember Jim hitting Jerry.

After my second son Bob was born, my husband got really nasty and I got very depressed. I was on better terms with my mother and I used to let her have the boys for the weekends to give me a break, but she only wanted Jerry. I remember when he was about two-and-half years old he stole my mother's purse and hid it. I wanted to smack him, but my mother wouldn't hear of it. She always spoilt him. He could get away with anything in her eyes.

I cannot remember hitting Jerry until he started playing truant from school. He could only have been about seven years old.

After I had my daughter, Jim and I got married. We moved at the end of that year, finally getting away from my mother. I had a new baby, a new house, and I thought things were finally going to be all right. It was around that time that I really became a battered wife. My children began to see more and more violence and they got quite out of hand, especially Jerry who was truanting and pinching things. I just didn't know how to handle it. I did give him a good hiding when I caught him playing truant, largely because he took his younger brother with him. Jerry was still only around seven, and his brother Bob was five. Jerry was very violent towards his brother; he blacked both his eyes, broke his teeth, and such like.

Bob used to fight all Jerry's battles for him. Jerry was timid and shy. He only really got out of hand when we moved and he got into trouble with the police. Then I really went over the top and I did give him a good hiding in the prison cell. He would then only have been 11 or 12 and had been picked up for stealing when he had enough money on him to buy the shoe laces, battery and toy gun he had stolen. He had also got Bob involved. They both had to attend court, but Jerry went out the next day and stole again, and was picked up again. Bob really cried, the court frightened him. But Jerry seemed to enjoy all the attention, and from then he seemed to go from bad to worse.

I never did tell my husband half of what happened. He was at sea most of the time. Bob would stick up for me when Jim got violent, but Jerry never would. He and his dad got on well; h was a different person when his dad was around. He always looked on Jim as his dad, and I never did find out who told Jerry about my rape. I know I never did. I think the discovery is to blame for his getting out of hand, and being in prison today.

Jerry's first supposed rape I still find hard to believe. He would have been fourteen years old. It was a very vicious attack. I remember reading about it in the paper and I was disgusted by it.

The first I knew about any of Jerry's rapes was when the police picked him up for an attack in the park behind where we lived. I couldn't understand why! He had a girlfriend and I thought he was finally going to settle down. I saw him at the police station and he just kept saying over and over again it wasn't him, it was the other one. He said half his head said it was him, and the other half didn't do anything.

I decided to stand by him and support him as best I could. The shock I felt cannot be explained. It was as though it wasn't really happening. I felt so alone, so twisted and hurt. I still find it hard to believe. I had no idea whatsoever that Jerry could ever be capable of rape or murder. It has taken me six years to come to terms with the fact that my son is someone I don't really know. I just wish he would talk to me. I wish I was able to understand why. I feel as though I am still being punished for keeping Jerry, and that is something I still cannot fully understand.

I try to do my best. I often wonder if my life has just been one mistake after another. I seem to have more time on my hands and I wonder if I am bitter. Having Jerry was the beginning of more problems than I could ever have imagined. I just wish I knew why, and I wonder when it will ever come to an end.

But I do know that Jerry is *my* son. I feel deeply responsible for everything he has done. In the beginning, when it first happened, I thought I would go crazy. But now, little by little, I am at least learning to like myself a bit more. And that's a start. I just want to help him all I can, but sometimes I feel it is beyond me. I feel like walking out and away from everything. I haven't yet learned to live with the stigma of having a rapist and murderer for a son.

Martin's experience

Sentenced to six months in prison for the indecent assault of his fiancée's neice, running concurrently with a charge of stealing for which he was sentenced to a further six months. He was out on parole after six months.

I was nine years old when someone at school told me I was adopted. I didn't know what it meant. I went home that day and asked my parents, 'Mummy, what does it mean to be adopted?' For the next hour or so I was told, 'We chose you,' 'You are very special,' 'To us, you are special.' And for the rest of the evening they wanted to make up for a past I knew nothing about. They gave me no background, no information about my real parents and suddenly, the person I thought I was just didn't exist any more. I no longer knew who I was. I felt like a plant whose roots had been stuck back in the ground, expected to grow and flourish.

The only thing we did know was that my sister and I had been adopted together. The family which we had come to know as our was never exactly what you would call close. We were fed and clothed and looked after but that was it. There was always so much missing: the ordinary, everyday kinds of things which other children took for granted. I can never remember playing football with my father, or him getting down on his hands and knees to play with our train set, or any of the other things you might expect a father to do. We were young teenagers before we were allowed out in the street to play. We could play in the back or the front garden, but that was it. Our friends would come to the wall and we could talk, but that was as far as it went.

After we found out that we were adopted, we had a craving to know more, to find out about ourselves and about our real roots

We tried to trace our real family. I got as far as getting my papers and saw my real name, but I was afraid to find out more; better the devil you know, kind of thing. My sister went further and found our real mother, at which point the adoption people admitted their mistake when it came to choosing our adoptive parents. In the days when we were adopted, adoption was so simple. They put the class of children with the same class of parents, and as long as they were earning money, they hoped that everything would work out right. But what we found increasingly was that as we tried to find our identity, the more lost we felt. We didn't know who we were any more. We hit an identity crisis, and the harder I tried to work things out in my mind, the worse it seemed to get.

I was nine years old when I caught polio, and I got a year behind at school. Polio took over the whole of my body, from the neck down. They said I was lucky in that, because I was young, I was very strong, and I'd just had my polio booster. Two other people caught the illness in the same week, and an old man of 69 died. We'd been swimming at a park, and after the outbreak, they closed it down.

For the first two days or so I kept being sick at school. Eventually, they sent me home. The doctor was called and at first diagnosed a bad cold. The next morning, I couldn't move. My eyes were the only working part of my body. I can't remember being scared, though. Everyone was being too nice and I was enjoying being the centre of attention. 'What can I get you?' 'Are you all right?' I only started being scared when I had injections in my spine. That is when I dreaded the next one coming the next day, because they hurt! I still get that feeling now down my back, and the panic I felt when it was about to happen.

School was kinder for a while when I went back, but the illness had put me back a class, and soon it was back to normal, being chased, being picked on, etc. It wasn't in me to fight, so I just took it all on board. My dad would say, 'Fight back. Defend yourself.' The one time I did the other boy fell through a window. I ended up with detention and a hiding from my mother when I returned home because my glasses were broken, the other boy had stamped on them before I pushed him through the glass. Dad tried to teach me to box with boxing gloves. He was a right one to teach me because he would bat me about the room himself if I didn't do anything just as he wanted me to. He had a very nasty temper and could throw me from one end of the room to the other. He would never discipline us without my mother's say-so, but when he did, we certainly knew about it! He'd knock you with one hand, and you'd look and see the other hand coming to receive you. A couple of kicks, and then your hair was grabbed hold of.

It was worse, much worse for my sister. She was slow. 'What's two and two, Jean?' 'Write 'the', Jean.' She couldn't. Because she couldn't or wasn't quick enough, she would catch it from my father.

At home, we weren't allowed out, we weren't allowed to meet other teenagers; we couldn't do this or that, and we just weren't given the opportunity to develop with people. Added to which, when our school initiated a programme of sex education they asked the parents' permission for their child to attend. Ours said a definite *no*, and because we couldn't then go to classes, we got laughed at by the other kids and spent that time in the library by ourselves, once a week for a period of 13 weeks. We weren't told anything at home, so we didn't find out anything. Sex for us became anything we chose it to be in our minds.

My sister and I tried to find out things between ourselves. We explored, we touched, and our parents' natural daughter joined in. She was in the same boat. Anything we found out, we were going to have to find out for ourselves. I don't mean we had intercourse or anything like that. We might play a game of cards, 'Strip Jack Naked', or something like that, and we would use the time to add to our education.

My sister reached 18 without knowing anything about sex, and she met this guy who she was very fond of, and they were happy together. They seemed to have found what it was about for them and they had something which worked.

One day, she phoned me at catering college to ask me to com home. She was going to tell our parents that they wanted to ge married. I said, 'Okay, sure', knowing my parents weren't enthusias tic. I arrived home, but she never came. She'd known whe our parents would be out, and she'd packed her bags and lef There was a terrible commotion! 'It's my life. I'm going t marry the man I love', was all she would say when they found he It came as a shock, I suppose, more so because she was suc a good and willing daughter. She had always tried to live t their rules. She was clean, tidy, hard-working. This would t the first time she would have openly defied them, but this w something she really wanted to do for herself.

I'd always wanted to join the Navy. My dad was all for it, but my mum said 'no', and that was that. Then when I decided on catering, suddenly there was all the encouragement and support in the world. 'Yeah, yeah. Good thing. Good job. Good prospects.' So in my last year at school, they let me go on day release to catering college and I worked towards my City and Guilds qualifications.

Relationships didn't come easy for me. Three or four times I tried to commit suicide. I became very unhappy, very lonely, and I didn't see the point of it all. What was the point when I had no one to share my life?

I was earning far more money than I could cope with. I just didn't know what to do. I started gambling, wasting it away. Then I had a relationship which went wrong. One thing came rapidly after another, and I lost interest in living, there was no real meaning to my life. I didn't feel loved, and I wasn't particularly needed by anyone. My idea of a good life is to work, to provide for your family. Having no family or any prospect of one in the forseeable future made life the bad dream that I couldn't cope with any more on my own. Gambling was a part of my seeking enjoyment, putting some zip back into my life.

I was so lonely. Every time there was a noise outside the window I'd rush to look outside. Out there was what it was all about, and I just wasn't a part of it anymore. I didn't have anyone there for me. Loneliness is a terrible feeling.

Because of my desperate need for companionship and to be needed, to be liked, I couldn't say no to anyone. When I was asked to put this girl up because I had a bigger place, I said, 'Yes, of course I wouldn't mind.' I didn't, then.

Joan was spotless, she was clean and tidy. She didn't like cooking, but then I loved that and because of catering experience it wasn't any problem.

Joan had been raped as a child by her brother, and consequently had a lot of problems. She was on invalidity benefit because she suffered from agoraphobia and depression. She drank, she was on Valium, and she couldn't go out. She wanted sex, but every time we tried, she would push me away, unable to go on. We had intercourse once in three years.

I could appreciate and sympathize with her problems. But after being led on, being teased, and then actually getting to that point of contact when it was all going to come together in bed, to be rejected just like that came hard. And God, was it frustrating! I would be aroused, and be drowned by all that feeling inside me. Masturbation was the only way I could let it go, to relieve the tension tying me up in knots inside. Cuddling and closeness, in the end, were enough for her. That was all that she could cope with because of her experience in the past, that was still so much a part of her today.

Living with Joan was hard, harder than anyone will ever know. We were two desperate people, one victim feeding off another. Her family had rejected her; we were alone in the world, except for each other. But then that wasn't enough the way things were, and our life got worse and worse and worse. If I was half an hour late home from work she would be down my throat. She was always drinking, and she would get violent, and take to me with a knife. Many times I was attacked and had to hold her down. She just went wild over the smallest things. Really it wasn't to do with today at all, she was still so affected by her past.

I started shoplifting. I was very good. My senses were keen, I was alert, and I could feel when it was right and when it was not. It was only if I was depressed and my senses weren't so acute that I got caught, as I did. Its the same if I gamble when I'm depressed, then I lose. We could come home with £2,000 worth of shoplifted goods some nights. The buzz comes when you know you've got away with it; it's a thrill. You're so tight, and your senses are so keen, thinking where to go out, and if you get caught, where to run, all the little things you have to think, to plan. All the time there is that eye in the back of your head; you know when someone is watching you. That's why, when you try stealing when you're depressed, the eye isn't so acute; its function is dulled. That's when you take a risk and you get caught.

In the past I've been caught, and it's always been probation. I've had it too easy. If I'd been hit harder in a lot of ways early on it would maybe have stopped me for the future. The risk would have got too great and it wouldn't have been worth it. As it was, I got caught twice. I was back shoplifting the next day. It took me about two hours to pluck up the courage to actually take the first thing, which was a newspaper, but once the buzz of having got away with it was there, then I was back to normal and it was the thrill of the chase which moved me on. That feeling is still with me, and every time I go into a shop I have to grit my teeth and buy what I've come in for, then walk away.

I've always wanted to be loved, I mean, really really loved. Loved for simply being me, without having to pretend to be someone else. One way or another I always arrive at the same cul-de-sac, finding out I've been used for whatever they can get out of me, or it's been on the rebound. But never parentwise, relationship-wise have I ever felt really, really loved.

Children love you, because they're so natural. They don't make demands, and they don't judge. They have no inhibitions, and you don't have to pretend, you can simply be yourself. It really is just as simple as that. That is the way it was with Joan's two nieces. It was a lovely feeling the way they used to fly through the door and dive into my arms. Kay was five and Isabel three.

They would come and stay at weekends and I was always buy-ing or shoplifting toys and planning treats. We'd play, and they'd ride on my back. Their mother is a single parent, so they'd missed out on Dad and I suppose I became a substitute. We were always babysitting and looking after them when their mum had to go out or away.

One day, Kay fell asleep in my arms. Within me was this over-whelming feeling of love and of being loved. It was a wonderful sensation, and I lost myself in the sensation and the emotion of that moment. It was something which I'd missed out on and was relishing now. Her clothing would keep going up and down as she wriggled and squirmed in her sleep. I kept pulling down her dress to cover her pants. Then up it would go again, and I'd pull it down. I really don't know why to this day, but one time when her dress went up, I touched her inside her knickers.

It's hard to put a feeling into words, and I cannot find a way to describe how I felt then, and I still don't know. I suppose that question will be always with me, unanswered. When it happened, I just know I was lost in this feeling of warmth and love and it felt so good.

Looking at it today, a year on, it was probably sexual because I just can't think of love without sex. So it did have that motive in it, I know. And that comes hard when I loved her, and she loved me. In that moment I forgot that she was a child.

All through my adolescent years I remember having the thought that you had to have sex before you can love somebody. I don't know where that came from, I just know that it was there.

Anyway, the following night we babysat again. Her mum was going out. I wasn't around, but Kay apparently said something then about what had happened the previous day when she was on my lap, so she couldn't have been totally asleep. She said, 'Martin touched me. Uncle Charles doesn't do that.'

It wasn't until a week later, when I was in the probation office, that the police suddenly came and arrested me. They said that accusations had been made, that I had interfered with a child, and that I was being arrested, etc. etc. and that anything I said would be taken down in evidence. I was in shock; I didn't know what to think. I loved that child, I really did.

They took me to the police station, interviewed me and I made a statement. I said in the statement that I didn't touch her in that way, I didn't interfere with her. There were two police officers in the room. While one was asking a question and I answered that question, the other was asking a question at the same time, and it all came down on me at once. In the end I really didn't know which question I was answering next. I felt twisted, inside and out. But I told them everything that happened; I had nothing to hide.

They charged me after typing everything out, and gave me a copy of my statement asking me to sign. I signed. I just wanted to get out, to get some fresh air and put my thoughts straight. When I read it, it didn't say what I had said. I asked my solicitor for the original written one that had been taken at the time, when I had been saying what had happened. But the typed one was the only one which was available and the one which went forward to the courts.

Three weeks on, I was in the Magistrates' Court, and they said that the child had an infection and bruising. My solicitor told the court that there was medical evidence to suggest that I was to blame for the infection. The child had had two medicals, one three or four days after the event by her GP, and the other ten days after by the police surgeon. Both were clear. They showed no bruising, no infection, no sign of sexual interference. Then there was a report by another GP three weeks on saying she had an infection, and the Social Services wondered where it had come from.

The case was taken to the Crown Court. I was charged with six months for that supposed offence, and two six months for shoplifting. I served six months, and came out on parole. I survived. In prison, they told me that if anybody asked, I was in for shoplifting, otherwise, it could have been bad. Other prisoners don't tolerate sex offenders.

While I was doing time, I got a lot of money back from my national insurance contributions. I couldn't have it in prison, so I arranged with the probation office to give it to my girlfriend for her to pay bills, etc. About £100 was kept in my account for when I came out. I said to my girlfriend, 'Use the rest to pay off two of my bills and the flat bills.' Okay, she agreed to that, but then she went out and drank the money until there was nothing left. She was having affairs, people were using her, and there was no end of trouble and problems with no one to see her right.

A week before I was due out, she went into a mental hospital voluntarily, and that's where she is today. I see her sometimes for a couple of hours at weekends. I can't just cut out my feelings for her, and I don't know what will happen to us in the future. We are an impossible combination and it can only ever lead to trouble. Only if she is willing to help herself can we ever have that chance. Obviously, because of the offence, I don't see Kay or Isabel any more. They moved away.

In the meantime, I'm trying to get my life together. I have a job, but I'm still lonely, nothing has really changed. One part of me still wants my girlfriend back, she's a companion, someone to share my life. She wants to finish but we hang on, and by hanging on, we could destroy what we have.

Martin's probation officer

We cannot take Martin and his offences in isolation. To help him we need to understand his life, his problems, the day-to-day way he leads his life, reaching out to include all those with whom he becomes involved.

We first made contact with Martin when he was given a probation order, and he came in to talk about his difficulties in his relationship with Joan, and how he and she would end up fighting. Things were becoming more and more agressive and they were coming to blows. He would end up hitting Joan and he didn't want to. He felt at that time it would help if Joan had someone to talk to as she was provoking the violence.

Joan is someone with whom Martin shared his life as common-law wife for three years prior to his imprisonment. Things were intolerable for them in the home and they wanted to know how to get close. The idea was to help them to set a time aside each evening for one another, to be close, to sit next to one another, and to simply get used to the idea of togetherness. Then, gradually, we tried to move them on towards touching, holding hands, giving each other a hug, with an absolute rule that there was to be no sexual touching. When they tried it, neither was able to carry it through. So impossible was it for them, that we didn't try it again.

We began working individually with Martin and Joan, concentrating initially on Joan because of her fear and ignorance about sex as a result of being raped by her brother. She also had other problems, like her disability — a bad cleft palate. During her first talk with us, her past experience came spilling out. To her knowledge, she was the only one in the family to be abused as she was, being picked on because she was different. Early learning difficulties made it easy for her to be labelled 'stupid' and she was sent to a special school. She had never really had the chance to learn about sex except by that awful painful experience. It was this rape, in later life, that was the underlying cause of her inability to live with Martin without the drinking, the fear, the violence, the self-harm, the abuse. What we didn't realize until quite a while later was that Martin himself carried into the relationship a similar set of problems and taboos.

Despite being articulate, Martin has quite a simplistic conception of his problems. He likes to think of himself in the role of the knight in shining armour. 'I am there to help.' 'She needs me.' He clings on to that. He gets a lot of kudos from being someone who can help others. The outcome is that it takes the heat off himself and his own fears and problems he still needs to confront. Within himself, he feels very inadequate, very insecure. But Martin is good in the role of 'helper', so he likes to be seen as helping, caring, capable. He fits them well, so why should he change or risk moving on to something else? He does have a genuinely warm and compassionate side to his nature. It isn't just that he needs to be *seen* in this role, but that he actually does belong. However, these emotions, this sense of belonging, all fall apart when he gets frustrated with Joan and with trying to make a relationship work.

The physical violence he has to contend with is high. I've taken a carving knife away from Joan, and she has knifed Martin in the home. Joan and I talked about today's violence in relation to the past, and she has agreed that knifing is an appropriate way to hurt somebody. But whether she is aiming hurt at Martin or her past abuser she is still not certain. She also does self-harm. Her wrists are covered in scars.

Martin's actual offence is confusing. We believe it was committed purely out of a sense of curiosity. During childhood, he was never given this opportunity to find out things in the normal way a child would find out; questions went unanswered. He was the eldest of four children, in a mixed marriage. His father was black and a GI airman. When he and his sister were adopted, the family in which he grew up were middle-class, straight-laced, and strict. He would learn nothing about real life issues or sexual attitudes there, other than what he could pick up along the way. Sex became the one issue not talked about, even to the extent that he and his sister were excluded from the sex education lessons at school.

Later, in his relationship with Joan, he was again prevented from gaining knowledge about sex because of Joan's own inadequacies and fear of being seen naked, being touched, and of intercourse. She would have to first get drunk to pluck up the courage to have sex, but then she would never get further than leading him on. At the point of physical contact everything would blow apart. Later, he would be left with bitter disappointment and frustration, while she became physically violent and threatening, fuelled by all the anger and frustration mainly directed at herself and her past abuser.

Martin was left as a frustrated and curious individual, fearful of rejection. When the child was on his lap, giving this unconditional love, he says he did not deliberately touch the child. He actually took off her knickers, but did not touch her genitals. He was curious to find out what she was all about. He would never knowingly hurt a child; he loves children.

I had a lot of anxieties about this case. When I went to the initial case conference and looked at the paperwork that came through, it was fairly obvious that the child had been examined and no damage had been found. Later she had been taken to the doctor by her mother, about one week after the event, and an infection, inflammation and bruising was found that couldn't actually have been caused by Martin. The doctor's report said that it was new and had occurred within the last couple of days. This tied in with the version that Martin had given at the time, that he had in no way physically injured her, although what he did is still a crime. The doctor went on to list out possible causes for the bruising and infection:

● That the child, then five years old, could have done it herself through masturbation

● That an adult could have abused her (but if not Martin, then who?)

What must be understood is that the family of the child over-reacted, by anyone's standards. They reacted very, very strongly. One other possible explanation that comes to mind is that the family may actually have set Martin up themselves by marking the child deliberately. They know nothing about Joan's experience: she has never discussed it with her family, and she has always believed that she was the only one involved. One issue she was frightened to tackle but which might have put her experience much more in perspective was if she had been able to confront her family, and particularly her brother, the abuser, with what had happened to her. Meanwhile, her sister and the rest of her family did not like Martin, and they wanted the relationship to end. However, they were not willing to offer Joan ongoing love and support.

As far as the offence is concerned, the family were there when it happened. Joan went into the kitchen leaving the child apparently asleep on Martin's lap and when she returned, the child still seemed to be asleep. If the child had been hurt or frightened, she would have cried out and her cry would have been heard. When Joan's sister came to collect her child, she told her mum in Joan's presence that it had happened. Mum hushed it up, and then arranged for Joan and Martin to babysit the next evening. It was quite a few days later when Joan came to see me at probation about it and later still before the child was examined by the doctor and things were put in motion.

What we are both saying quite strongly as probation officers concerned with both Martin and Joan is that Martin's account is by and large accurate, and that the crime was committed out of a sense of curiosity more than anything else.

The abuser profile

Eddy Burfitt, Senior Probation Officer, Northumbria, talks about the personality profile of the abuser

Probation officers usually find that those found guilty of offences of dishonesty and physical violence can normally admit to the facts of their behaviour, its wrongfulness and the implications for the victim. Sex abusers are often quite unable to do so, or at the very least are only able to acknowledge part of the truth under pressure.

Truth hurts, the more so, it seems, for sex offenders, whether they are someone who is indecently exposing themselves, or a rapist using weapons and dire threats. The abuser has the greatest difficulty facing the truth of his intentions, his actions and the consequences for his victims, however obvious these may appear to be to those concerned. This block is likely to persist and remain strong, making it difficult for the offender to help himself or to be helped by others, leaving him vulnerable to commit further offences for as long as it lasts.

An abuser who has pleaded guilty in court is often remanded on bail for probation officers to prepare social inquiry reports. He will be asked about the circumstances of the offence and his attitude to it. The account that many give is so devoid of incriminating behaviour as to contradict the guilty plea already made. Seeking an explanation invites the assertion that the abuser is protecting somebody by their actions, perhaps the young victim, from giving evidence. The offender is apparently some kind of sacrificial victim of the criminal justice system. If, instead, we ask for permission to see a copy of the abuser's police statement, he will almost certainly consent, knowing that it contains a frank and sufficient statement of guilt which he will not deny again.

He has helped us toward the truth, but he cannot bear to acknowledge it by speaking it at this point.

Sex offences cause people a greater degree of revulsion than any other. Life in prison provides many reminders of that. Known rapists and child molesters are constantly subjected to every kind of verbal and physical filth, whilst facing an everpresent threat of physical attack. Many elect for the voluntary segregation of Rule 43, which affords physical protection whilst increasing stigma and verbal abuse.

Abusers do not try to justify sexual offending in general. They appear to be as genuinely revolted by it as the rest of us, perhaps the more so. Many have themselves been the victims of sexual, physical and mental abuse. To offend, it is necessary for them to re-order the truth, to manipulate and distort it until the situation is inverted. What happened may not be in dispute, but subjective interpretation will distort refusal into permission, fearful acquiescence to enthusiastic co-operation, and rape into seduction.

In working with abusers, it is easy to be made to feel that if only the abuser can convince you that others misinterpreted the situation, not him, then he will be relieved of his guilt. Underneath, however, there usually lies a realization of truth which feeds self-revulsion and the fear of total rejection by family and by society, as well as the fear of being a rampaging monster who will in future prey on men, women and children in an uncontrolled way. Underneath is a person of normal sexual desires which demand satisfaction or control. Sexual offenders are likely to be socially gauche, too shy or inept to 'eye up' and 'chat up' girls, ignorant of signals to 'come on' or 'back off'.

Many sex offenders are sent to prison, an assured protection for others as long as the sentence lasts, arguably a deterrent to other potential abusers and a demonstration of society's view of such behaviour. It is a matter of some concern, however, that long prison sentences may do little to ensure that the abuser will not continue his abuse once he is free to do so. In prison, he will see very few women, but those he does see may become objects of his sexual fantasies. There is no limit to imagination stimulated by the talk of sexually deprived people, ubiquitous soft porn, and frequent masturbation.

Abusers do not admit their offences to fellow prisoners, a wise safety precaution, but one prohibiting vernacular help. Prison staff will avoid stigmatizing sex offenders and putting them at risk. Probation officers and psychologists in the prison are insufficient in number for work with other than a minority of the many abusers. Many abusers can serve their sentences as if they had never committed a sexual offence, pretending that it is for something else that they are imprisoned, not sharing their guilt and disturbance, helped by all to bury the truth in fantasy and distortion.

Fortunately, there are grounds for hope. Group therapy of the kind seen at Grendon Underwood prison clearly helps abusers, not only to face the truth and themselves, but to have confidence for the future. Ray Wyre, ex-prison probation officer, is pioneering new structural approaches to working with sex offenders. Lifeline, a national charity helping victims of domestic violence, is providing a counselling service which offers hope, not only for the victim, but also for the abuser, who, if he can be helped and enabled to face the pain of the truth, should be able to prevent himself hurting others in the future.

Breaking the circle

Hilary Eldridge, Probation Officer with Nottingham Probation service

Most people when asked the question 'Should we try to stop sex offenders committing further offences?' would be likely to answer 'Yes, of course'. However, when we ask 'What should be done?' many answers emerge and controversy rages. 'Lock them up', 'Castrate them', 'Find out why they do it', 'Teach them to make normal adult sexual relationships.'

As a new probation officer starting work with sex offender clients some 13 years ago, I had to ask myself 'What would be the most effective means of preventing offenders from finding more victims, who would have to go through the life sentence of misplaced guilt and misery which is so often the lot of sexually abused people?'

In the cases of some sex offenders, the only answer may be to lock them up. Some people are too dangerous to be allowed their freedom. However, the vast majority of sex offenders are locked up for periods of time ranging from a few months to several years. At some point they are released, and it is therefore reasonable to ask what effect prison has on the likelihood of reoffending.

Incarceration in prison usually has the effect of encouraging sex offenders to deny their offending almost to the point where it gets lost in legend. In prison, sex offenders are viewed as the bottom of the pile by other prisoners. The risk of being beaten and assaulted is high, and so it is not usually in their interests to identify themselves as sex offenders and talk honestly about their behaviour. Some prisons have groups for sex offenders, but these usually cater for only a small number of abusers, and do little more than scratch the surface in attempting to confront and modify what may be the habits of an offender's lifetime.

Most sex offenders are released from custody with the same attitudes, beliefs and behaviour patterns they possessed when sentenced. The road to further offending remains open. On its own, fear of a return to prison is unlikely to break the addictive cycle of a sex offender. An alcoholic or drug abuser may at least have had the benefit of a break from alcohol or drugs. The sex offender has had plenty of time to rehearse his offending through sexual fantasy in masturbation.

Castrating sex offenders, both literally and chemically, is often talked about. However, castration doesn't address the distorted attitudes which may have led to offending. Much sex offending is essentially the sexualization of violence and is about power as well as sex. Castration cannot solve those problems and may exacerbate them.

Sex offenders often say 'I want to see a psychiatrist to find out why I do it.' Finding out a single reason for sex offending is a very difficult task. Even if one finds an important pointer, for example, if the offender was sexually abused as a child, this does not help the offender to change. It can simply become a new excuse. Insight does not of itself promote change.

Both sex offenders themselves and those who comment on sex offending often say that if the offenders had regular sex with an adult partner, they would not offend. However, experience of working with sex offenders shows that fathers do not rape their children just because their sexual relationships with their wives are poor, nor do men assault women simply because they are not having regular sex.

Sex offending is a complex phenomenon. There are many competing individual and environmental explanations for its persistence. However, work with sex offenders both in Britain and America has shown that a multi-causal analysis may be most helpful. David Finkelhor in his work on child sex abuse suggests that four conditions need to be fulfilled before such abuse can occur. Firstly, there has to be someone who has the motivation to abuse. Secondly, that person has to find ways of overcoming his internal inhibitors, or conscience, which may prevent him from acting out his wishes. Thirdly, the abuser has then to overcome any external inhibitors, that is, the people who may stop him from carrying out his wishes. Fourthly the abuser has to overcome the child's resistance.

There are individual and societal explanations which may help us understand how an abuser reaches the point of assaulting a child. Abusers come from a wide variety of social backgrounds and life experiences, hence no single explanation can be made to fit every case. All the theories which relate to child sexual abuse can be grouped as possible contributors to each of the four conditions. Within this framework different explanations can be seen to fit different abusers. The framework has been applied principally to child sexual abuse, but we have found it a useful way of analysing sexual attacks on adults as well.

In the Nottinghamshire Probation Service we have run courses and groups for sex offenders for a number of years. We have worked with people whose ages range from early 20s to late 60s, and who have raped and abused adults and children. At first sight they appear to be a very mixed group. There have been paedophilic stepfathers and 'uncles' who have sought out families with children. Some have been fathers who have raped the adolescent daughters who look like their mothers but are less assertive. There have been patriarchs who have used sex to control and subdue several generations of family members, sometimes of both sexes. Some abusers have been highly intelligent people, and others have been on the border of subnormality. Some are nervous, socially isolated people who are afraid of adult friendships. Some have used gratuitous violence to force their victims to submit, whilst others have used persuasion based on exploitation of their relationship with the victim. Some have used alcohol and substance abuse to overcome their inhibitions, and others have persuaded themselves they were simply teaching the victim about sex.

Despite these differences we have found that sex offenders do have much in common with each other. Our own observations are largely supported by current thinking in the field of sex offender treatment. The work of Derek Perkins and Ray Wyre in Britain, and Steven Wolf in America has indicated that convicted sex offenders may share certain characteristics and exhibit predictable behaviour patterns. In many cases poor self-image, coupled with a tendency to interpret anything in relation to self is observed. This is often linked to very poor social perception skills — a tendency to experience rejection where it doesn't exist, and to project feelings, often sexual ones, on to others. Highly distorted attitudes towards women and children and unusual thinking and logic patterns are prevalent.

Given these characteristics, sex offenders are highly vulnerable to environmental influences conducive to sex offending. Men, for example, may be influenced by the representation of women as sex objects in the media. On a more individual level the abuser may come from a family background where sexual boundaries were weak; they may have been abused themselves. Not surprisingly, difficulties in making relationships of any depth are frequently found.

Non-sex offenders may have similar problems, but sex offenders are different in that these characteristics are usually linked to extreme sexual preoccupation and a sexual arousal system which includes very strong arousal to some illegal activity, for example, violent sex or sex with children and adolescents.

Many rehearse their offending several times a day in masturbation. After committing an offence they masturbate thinking of what they did and what they may do another time, thus reinforcing their addiction to the behaviour and increasing the likelihood of repetition.

An addictive cycle is often well developed in sex offenders. For example, a man who is predisposed to sex offending because of his personality and sexual arousal patterns, faces a stress point in his life. He responds to this by seeking solace in masturbation. Rehearsal of an offence takes place in masturbation fantasy and a target victim is identified. He finds ways of overcoming his inhibitions to offending, for example, he uses alcohol or drugs. He prepares the environment so that any external inhibitors, for example, the presence of other people, are excluded. The victim whom he has targetted is subjected to a sexual assault. The offender then masturbates about the assault, thus reinforcing his sexual obsession with it. He may suffer brief guilt, but always manages to push this away by denying harm to the victim, denying responsibility, or denying that he will ever do it again. If the cycle is not broken, he will probably repeat the process and commit further offences.

Addictive cycles certainly exist in the lives of many people, and may cause problems. For instance they may centre around alcohol or drug abuse, or compulsive gambling. In the case of sex offenders preoccuption with sexual fantasy and the process of carrying this through to reality often forms the centre of their world. There is very high under-reporting of sexual offences, and hence the offenders who come to our notice may be at the point of first conviction, but they are rarely first offenders.

Most sex offenders know their behaviour is socially unacceptable and at times experience feelings of shame and self-loathing. They have discovered through experience that they will be more easily accepted and they more easily accept themselves if they pretend the offence was an aberration, or that they weren't responsible because they were drunk, or the victim led them on, or they only did it once, or they didn't do it at all.

People working with sex offenders know that denial is the biggest obstacle. If the worker does not know or cannot face offenders' characteristics and the way in which they operate, she or he is prevented from effectively confronting their denial and helping them to move forward. Sex offenders are experts at using techniques of neutralization to enable them to continue offending. Failure to challenge the offender's version of events is dangerously collusive. The offender perceives it as legitimizing his attitudes and he draws it into his hidden world as licence to continue thinking and behaving in ways which increase the risk of sexual reoffending.

In Nottinghamshire Probation Service we have developed structures within which denial can be confronted and the offender's passive version of events can be challenged. A period of concentrated work is available for clients of the service who have committed sexual offences against children and/or adults. This takes the form of a two-week full-time course which often has tremendous impact on its members. Follow-up work can take place at individual probation officer/client meetings and through attendance at a small open ended weekly group for sex offenders. Attendance at both the course and the group is voluntary. Despite the confronting nature of the work, we are rarely short of referrals. Seven people attended the last course voluntarily, and completed each day without fail. The weekly group currently has nine members, most of whom attend every session.

The principal aim of our work is to help sex offenders develop strategies to prevent themselves from reoffending. They learn more about their offending patterns and the cycles of behaviour which perpetuate offending. They begin to identify the triggers which start the cycle, the way in which an offence can be rehearsed through fantasy, the point at which offending is likely to take place, and the way repeated offending is reinforced by their behaviour patterns. They learn ways of interrupting these cycles, and finding positive escape routes at the earliest points.

We encourage offenders to examine their own sexual arousal and to consider how this might be controlled or modified. Attitudes and thinking patterns affect the development of internal inhibitors which may act to prevent reoffending, so ideas and attitudes about women and children are discussed and frequently challenged. The use of language which objectifies women for example, 'There's a nice bit of skirt, I'd like to give that one', is constantly confronted. There is also a strong emphasis on gaining a more realistic understanding of the way victims feel and of the consequences of sexual assault for the offenders' own victims.

Video and audio tapes in which victims describe how they felt when they were attacked and how it has affected them in later life are shown. Offenders often say in self defence, 'She/he didn't stop me; didn't scream; didn't run away.' When they begin to acknowledge that the victims may have been frightened for their lives, they begin to understand that the victim's response can never be accepted as an excuse for the offender's behaviour.

Offenders frequently describe their behaviour in terms that would suggest they are themselves the victims of their own victim's unreasonable behaviour. For example, 'She/he led me on. How was I to know she/he didn't want sex?' We use behaviour-specific questioning to analyse the offence in detail and discover what actually did lead up to it. This usually succeeds in moving the offender from a passive to a more active version of events. Most offenders go through a stage where they make what I would describe as interim statements. These statements admit some level of responsibility, but still suggest the victim's complicity. Some of the statements made by offenders in this book fall into this category. They suggest that real movement has started, but there is still a long way to go. Repeated detailed analysis of an offence enables the offender's version to be constantly challenged.

There are many ways in which a victim's resistance can be overcome. These might include statements to both adult and child victims such as, 'I'll kill you if you don't', 'I won't hurt you if you'll just let me have sex', 'I'll tell your husband/wife/mother/father what you've been doing with me if you don't', 'You wore a short skirt, it's your fault', 'It's only natural, any normal person would do it', 'If you really love me you'll do it'. Gradually offenders begin to see how they controlled their own victims, and either prevented them from saying 'No', or failed to hear them say 'No'.

During the courses and groups, offenders often confront each other's behaviours and attitudes. All sex offenders share a vested interest in keeping their offences secret. It is only in the presence of people who have committed similar offences that they can feel safe enough to share thoughts and experiences which have hitherto remained secret and oppressive. This break from isolation encourages a break with past denials which have hindered change. For example, there is less pressure to pretend that 'It only happened once', 'It'll never happen again', 'It was just the drink', and so on.

Sex offenders are the experts and are very quick to challenge denial in each other. Group pressure can be very strong, and during the two-week, full-time course it becomes increasingly difficult for people to keep up a pretence. Daily challenge and confrontation not just by probation officers but by other sex offenders is very effective in breaking down denial. The work is often hard and painful for the participants but the group experience helps them begin to face the reality of their behaviour and their own responsibility for it, and move forward to take responsibility for change.

Our work with sex offenders in Nottinghamshire looks promising, but at present it reaches a relatively small number of sex offenders surpervised by the service, and follow-up to the courses and groups is not always sufficient to be effective. Staff are professional and enthusiastic, and management is sympathetic, but there are many constraints which operate to make the work less effective than it could be.

The probation service itself is constrained by the wide range of demands made upon limited resources. Probation officers are generic workers who usually operate in geographically based field teams, and are expected to supervise a diverse clientèle who commit offences ranging from petty shoplifting to murder. One of their primary functions, which takes priority over others, is the provision of social enquiry reports on demand of the courts.

Increasingly, the probation service is being required to provide control in the community. Such control can lead to a greater emphasis on a client actually reporting regularly and frequently, rather than on the quality of the work done with that client when he or she does report.

The strength of denial in sex offenders means that effective work takes a lot of time. There is no short cut. If progress is made, it needs reinforcement over a long period if it is to be maintained. There is a clear mismatch between the work required to be effective, and the resources currently available.

In the case of child sex abuse within the family, there is a strong case for saying that the various agencies involved should work together. A coherent approach is frequently prevented because the agencies have different priorities; have differing demands made upon them, and identify different people as their clients. For example, one scenario might be that the Social Services Department may take the view that the child will be safe from further sexual abuse by the father if the child is taken into care and not allowed to see the abusing parent. The probation officer, who according to her or his terms of employment, has the role of 'advising, assisting and befriending' the offender, may support that person in seeking access to the child through the courts. Hence the two agencies may enter into a head on collision. Meanwhile, the offender and child may meet secretly without the consent or knowledge of either agency!

Not all children who have been sexually abused are clear that they never want to see the offender again. Some are highly confused, and although they hated the abuse and wanted it to stop, they nevertheless wanted that person as a parent. A child may say, 'I wanted him to stop, but I still wanted him to be my daddy.' Some children carry enormous misplaced guilt because they didn't keep the abuse a secret. They feel they are responsible for breaking up the family, or that it was something about them that attracted the abuse. The offender was their parent. They can't write him off as safely out of the way. Their pain and confusion continues.

Good inter-agency co-operation can and has helped families make sense of and survive what has happened to them. Joint work can be done to assess risk and the appropriateness or not of family rehabilitation. Account can be taken of the needs and wants of the individual family members. The vital ingredients are first that all the workers should identify protection of the abused child as their primary role, and secondly that sufficient time is allowed for the work. Again there is a clear mismatch between the type or work needing to be done, and the resources available to do it.

The lack of resources leads me to pose the question 'Does society really want to do anything constructive about sexual abuse?' This is the land of mixed messages. In the area of child sex abuse, social workers are accused of being neglectful if they do not identify situations where there is sexual abuse, but woebetide them if they do find it. At the least they can consider themselves to be over zealous, at worst family wreckers and child abusers.

The mixed messages are easy to understand. Yes, I want abused children to be able to speak out and be protected, but the double-edged sword is that the sex offender might be my husband/father/brother/neighbour or a mother or sister.

Adult sexual abuse is similarly riddled with mixed messages. Sex offenders often view women as perfect untouchable madonnas, or whores who are asking to be abused. This is only an extreme reflection of society's views about women, especially those often put forward in the media.

Courts make statements about women having contributed more or less to their own rape. The behaviour of the victim seems at times to affect the length of sentence imposed on the offender. Hence, if as a woman you are literally too frightened to move, or you decide you're less likely to be murdered if you co-operate, your abuser may get a shorter sentence than he would if you risked life and limb by attempting to fight someone much stronger than yourself! When someone robs a bank or steals from a Post Office, no one expects that they will receive a shorter sentence because the clerk handed over the money! Similarly the clothes women wear have been used to justify such comments as 'She asked for it, dressing like that.' The view that men with erections require immediate orifices to put them into, and that it is the responsibility of women to ensure that they do not provoke or allow themselves to be alone with such erections, is common in society.

Effective work with sex offenders has to counter and challenge views such as these constantly. Sex offenders are expert in finding justifications, rationalizations and excuses for their behaviour. It is a very real problem that our society is so good at supporting them in this. The relegation of other human beings, be they men, women or children, to the status of sex objects, is in my experience, one of the most crucial factors in sex offending. If society is serious about wanting to reduce sex offending, then this area has to be addressed not just by professional social workers and by sex offenders, but by everyone. If it is not, then more and more victims will continue to receive life sentences of fear, shame and suffering.

PART FOUR
Recovery

Every time my husband comes near me and wants to make love, I cringe at him touching me. I feel disgusted and dirty, I wish I could understand my true feelings, but everything is kept bottled up inside. Even though I have told my husband how I feel, and he does try very hard to understand, it doesn't help to change my feelings about it. If only I could love him sexually I feel we could make our marriage work.

Susan

I am ashamed to be a woman. From a small age I remember my father touching and hurting me. I thought I had buried these memories until I married three years ago and had to sleep with John, my husband. When he touches me now, it is like my father all over again. When my father would force me to sleep with him I felt so dirty. Now I have carried those feelings with me into marriage.

Anne

I suffered sexual abuse from my elder brother. Now I have dark periods when I get depressed to the point of suicide. I cannot see the point of carrying on. I burn and cut myself frequently. My problem started when I was about seven, and ended on my thirteenth birthday when my periods began and he was afraid I would become pregnant. Now I cannot make a relationship; all the time I am afraid of what men will do. I find I am very much living with the pain of the past.

Sarah

Why me? I'm a capable, hard-working woman with a full-time job, a nice house, a loving husband, and a dear little girl. Yet, when I come under stress, I find pictures from the past interfering with today, so much so that I cannot afford to relax lest my feelings get the better of me. I feel as if I am going mad.

My trouble stems from my relationship with my mother. I was never a child; I became whatever my mother wanted me to be. I became the whipping boy — threatened, abused, hurt. I remember making the fire, and crying because it wouldn't take. I received a kick so hard in my back that I couldn't stand. Today, I am still having treatment. Now I want to break out, to be free, to find myself and be me.

Lisa

Hope

John Hodge, clinical psychologist

The experiences documented in this book are unfortunately by no means unique. It is becoming clear that physical and sexual abuse is much more common than we would wish or are able to accept. Changes in social attitudes, perhaps initially triggered by the feminist movement, but now with a momentum all their own, have made it increasingly possible for people to come forward and divulge their experiences with the expectation of a sympathetic hearing. Public awareness of the extent of physical and sexual abuse of both adults and children has been raised and continues to be raised by the activities of such groups as Women's Aid, Rape Crisis Centres, Lifeline and by an increasing number of magazine articles, television programmes, and books such as this. This awareness is beginning to affect legislation about how victims — especially children — are treated in court, and also beginning to influence attitudes about what constitutes appropriate sentencing of offenders

Professional attitudes towards physical and sexual abuse have also undergone recent changes. Previously, there was a tendency for professionals to view reports of abuse with scepticism unless there was irrefutable evidence, such as physical damage. This attitude was perhaps most evident in the courts where it has long been recognized that obtaining a conviction for rape in the absence of clear signs of assault was very difficult. However, scepticism has also been the hallmark of other professional groups whose responsibility it is to provide care. General practitioners, psychiatrists, psychologists and social workers have all been very slow to recognize the occurrence and extent of the problem. Perhaps part of the reason for this slowness to recognize the reality of the problem dates back to Sigmund Freud, whose work has been very influential in shaping professional attitudes this century. Although some of Freud's patients told him of experiences of sexual abuse, the pervading moral climate of the time made it impossible for him to believe them. Probably in order to reconcile the patients' accounts with this moral climate, he went on to develop some of the key features of his theory of psychoanalysis on the assumption that these experiences of abuse were not only imaginary but evidence of unconscious wish-fulfilment. In doing so he set the trend for other professionals to follow suit.

While scepticism is being replaced by awareness, professional workers are facing the dilemma of how to react to the increasingly overwhelming evidence of prevalent abuse of both adults and children. Some over-react, as probably happened recently in the North East of England, leading to the Cleveland inquiry. In this case it seems likely that the incidence of child abuse was probably over diagnosed and the response of the Social Services probably too precipitate. Over-reactions such as this can have catastrophic effects on the family relationships of the innocent parties involved. However, the effect may also be to mask the true extent of abuse and to draw attention away from the victims of genuine abuse. On the other hand, events such as occurred in Cleveland do encourage public debate, not only about the extent of abuse, but also about the inadequacy of response.

Other professionals react to the emerging evidence of the prevalence of abuse by trying to categorize the problem so that they can respond from within their repertoire. The most obvious example of this is when victims are prescribed drugs, not to help them overcome the immediate, traumatic effects of an episode of abuse itself, but rather in some way to 'cure' them of the abuse that may have happened many months or years ago. Drugs have a poor record in helping people to overcome the long-term effects of psychological trauma. When they fail to be effective, the professional worker can often feel helpless, and react by either continuing to prescribe drugs or, in some cases becoming angry at the victim as being in some way responsible for their ineffectiveness.

Given the relatively recent recognition of the extent of the problem by the professional and scientific community, it is perhaps not surprising that systematic help for victims is in its infancy. We are only just beginning to discover what kinds of short- and long-term effects abuse has on victims. Since abuse victims are all individuals with different backgrounds and experiences, it is therefore not surprising that abuse affects them in many different ways. Abuse, itself, can occur in many different ways and over many different time scales. It may have different effects on people whether it occurs to them as children or as adults. Victims are by no means always women or young girls; male victims are also more common than we have realized until recently.

The chapters in this book reflect many of the problems that can be the consequence of being abused as well as some of the many, many ways in which abuse can occur. Victims often feel alone and unique, not only for having been abused, but also in terms of the effects that the abuse has had on them. Since many are unable to divulge their experiences of abuse, even to close friends or family, reactions of others to their distress can often be unsympathetic and impatient. This, in turn, can lead to further problems as the victim feels more and more isolated and more and more desperate to expunge the experiences from memory. When a person has had a traumatic experience, such as abuse, it is usually very important that they be given the opportunity, as soon as possible, to work through the emotional upheaval. When this is not possible, as, for example, when they are unable to confide in anyone, then the emotional distress can become long-term. Perhaps the most common example of this is after someone dies. Very often it is the person who seems to cope best immediately after the bereavement, the one who seems strongest and on whom everyone else depends at that time, who takes longest to come to terms with their grief. The same kinds of rules apply to people who have undergone traumatic abuse. If they have to suppress the experience in the short term, they are more likely to run the risk of long term emotional distress. Why this is so is not clear at the present time.

It seems that the more desperate the individual is to escape or avoid the memories of what has happened the more and more difficult to deal with and paradoxically more insistent and more persevering they become. Instead of becoming less distressed over time, for some, distress can seem to grow and overwhelm. This doesn't always happen, of course. People are individuals and individuals react differently. The experience of abuse is very different for some than for others, and is not necessarily always traumatic. The consequences of abuse can be very different. Most victims probably come to terms with their experiences, at least in part, without the need for professional help. It is the others, those who never seem to be able to come to terms with what has happened to them, who become most disabled.

The variety of effects of abuse is immense. As with adults, where the victim is a child, there can be considerable individual variation in outcome. At their worst, short-term effects can encompass sleep and eating disturbances, bedwetting, school problems (for example, truancy), behavioural disturbances of all types, especially those involving fear and aggression or antisocial behaviour, inappropriate sexual behaviour for their age and, on occasion, self-injury. Many of these problems as well as other, more long-term effects such as depression, anxiety and tension, nightmares, fear of men and fear of darkness, can last into adulthood. The list doesn't stop there. Other consequences can also be very long-lasting, including low self-esteem, poor interpersonal relationships and social functioning — even passivity — or alternatively, difficulty in controlling anger. Effects on sexual functioning can also persist, and in adulthood often can take the form of dissatisfaction with sexual enjoyment, vaginismus or dyspareunia (pain during intercourse). One particularly worrying feature is that victims of early sexual abuse also seem to be especially prone to being victimized again at some later stage in their life, either by partners or others. This may be because they fail to learn ways of coping with or recognizing situations in which they are vulnerable. (Those interested in a more detailed description of the effects of abuse on children should read *A Sourcebook On Child Sexual Abuse*. See Bibliography, p. 200).

Adult victims of abuse can suffer the same range of emotional, social and sexual consequences of abuse as children. For some adults, as well as children, the effects may well be tempered by well-developed social and familial relationships which may serve to buffer the victim to some extent. This will be the case especially if the partner or family reacts in a sympathetic and supportive manner. However, where the abuse occurs within a marital or family relationship, the effects can be very long-term and disabling, even after the victim has effected an escape.

These various possible outcomes of abuse can also result from experiences other than abuse and not all victims experience th full range of these consequences. Some experience little aftermath, especially where the abuse may have occurred without fear or trauma. Others seem to experience almost the whole range of distress. Most victims are affected by some consequence for some amount of time following the abuse. Each has her own particular pattern of response to the abusive experience and we are a long way from understanding in detail why some should be affected in one or other ways while others suffer quite different problems. The probable reasons most likely lie within the individual's unique experience of abuse interacting with previous life experiences and coping strengths and weaknesses. However, understanding why a particular individual reacts as she or he does may be less important than being able to offer help. This can often consist, in the first instance, of breaking down the totality of the reaction into manageable chunks. Very often victims are so overwhelmed by their total experience of distress that they are unable, by themselves, to break it down into components which they can begin to learn to cope with.

While each individual has their own, unique pattern of reactions to having been abused, some particular reactions seem to occur more commonly and cause more difficulty. I would like to examine one or two of these and to give examples of some of the ways professionals may be of some help to victims. As already indicated, professional response is still in its infancy and there are by no means solutions to all the problems consequent on sexual abuse. However, some kinds of approach do seem to be showing some promise for some kinds of problems. It must be emphasized, however, that professionals by no means always (or even often) agree as to the best kind of help to offer. What will be described here is one kind of approach which some current research seems to support. This research comes mainly from the psychological literature and so those presently most likely to be able to offer the kinds of help described are more likely to be clinical psychologists. Unfortunately not all clinical psychologists work in the same way, so for victims interested in these forms of help, it may be necessary to shop around. The particular type of psychological approach I will describe is usually called Behaviour Therapy, sometimes Cognitive-Behaviour Therapy. It is available on the National Health Service, mainly from clinical psychologists, but is also practised by some doctors, nurses and social workers. A final word of warning, however. Even behaviour therapists are not all conversant with the problems and consequences of physical and sexual abuse. Although public and professional awareness is increasing all the time, this is still often viewed as a very specialized area of work.

One common problem experienced by victims is feelings of panic and anxiety which were associated with the trauma of the abuse when it occurred. This is particularly the case where the abusive incidents have been associated with strong fear or disgust. In such cases it can happen that otherwise innocuous experiences and circumstances surrounding the abusive episodes can become associated with the abuse itself and later trigger memories or flashbacks to these episodes. These flashbacks are often accompanied by intense fear or panic. It is quite common for this type of reaction to occur within a relatively short period after the abusive episode. However, it can become a prolonged problem for some victims and be very disabling. The more often abuse has occurred and the more prolonged the period of abuse, the more cues can be associated with it to trigger these unpleasant memories.

The natural reaction is to try to avoid these triggers and to block off the memories when they can't be avoided. On occasion this can be so successful that amnesia, complete loss of memory, may occur for the incident or period of abuse, but this rarely lasts indefinitely. Unfortunately avoidance doesn't always work and as time goes by, the victim becomes less and less confident in their ability to cope with these memories and can become all the more distressed by them. The flashbacks become more vivid and apparently more uncontrollable and avoiding them or keeping them at bay begins to dominate each day. As strategies for avoidance or escape fail to work, the victim can become more and more depressed, worsening the feelings of intense helplessness associated with the memories.

There are probably a number of ways of overcoming these problems, each suitable to different degrees of severity of the problem. There are now a number of 'anxiety-management' techniques available which can do much to bring the intolerable levels of anxiety and fear under control. These range from simple relaxation training to more sophisticated versions combining breathing control training with cognitive or mental self-contro techniques. These various techniques have been shown to be effective in a wide range of anxiety and panic related problems and will also work for those associated with abuse.

Most behaviour therapists would probably introduce their client to some method of anxiety control and then gradually teach them to deliberately cope with the different cues which may set off the flashbacks or anxiety attacks. In some cases, especially where there is a wide range of cues involved, clients may be taught to cope with the flashbacks or panic attacks themselves. By doing this, the client can sometimes be helped to progress much more quickly than otherwise. While this treatment is not comfortable, it is always less distressing than clients imagine it to be. A client who has been avoiding cues and memories for some time almost always suffers more from the anxiety associated with anticipating these memories than that associated with the memories themselves. The main point to remember is that lack of treatment is not comfortable either, and the discomfort is much more indefinite than that associated with treatment.

As an example of how this approach may be used, let us imagine the case of a victim who subsequently complains of sexual problems with their partner. They may say that whenever they attempt intercourse now, they experience a flashback of the abuse experience, and that intercourse is consequently both difficult and painful. These flashbacks have persisted over a period of months or years and have resulted in serious disruption of sexual enjoyment.

In a case such as this, assuming no other complications, it is likely that the client would respond to the type of treatment already outlined. Firstly, they may be taught a method of anxiety management, in this case deep muscle relaxation may well be appropriate. If the victim had complained more of panic then a different anxiety management technique may have been more appropriate. Once they had mastered relaxation, a way would have to be found to teach the victim to use it to control the anxiety associated with the flashback. Since, in this case, flashbacks are most often triggered by intercourse, an indirect method of creating a flashback would need to be found. In many cases this would simply involve asking the victim to relate the abuse experience. If this is not possible, or too distressing, it is almost certain that some other cue associated with the abusive episode will be able to be found which will trigger some part of the flashback. The client is then taught to use their new skills in anxiety management, and practice allows the victim to control the anxiety associated with the flashback. This in itself may not entirely resolve the sexual problem (although in some cases it would), but it would enable any other treatment necessary to be much more effective. A major attraction of this approach is that the client develops new skills to bring their problem under their own control. In most cases, the flashbacks will gradually die away and cause little more trouble, but where they may come back briefly (say during a period of unusual stress), the client has a method of dealing with them which will prevent them becoming a major problem again.

This is a simple example of a single problem resulting from abuse. Where abuse has been prolonged, victims often complain of spontaneous flashbacks. In these cases, several different memories and their associated cues may require to be tackled in this way. Once the memories have been dissociated from the intense anxiety, the frequency and duration of spontaneous flashbacks and memory intrusions is considerably reduced.

It is seldom, however, that this particular treatment approach will be sufficient in itself to eliminate all the consequences of abuse. It is a specific technique which works well with consequences associated with fear and anxiety. It may have some positive effect on depression, by allowing greater freedom of action. It is unlikely to influence other problems which do not have their roots in fear, such as those associated with guilt or self blame.

The tendency for victims to blame themselves in some way is a common problem resulting from abuse. Often they berate themselves, in hindsight, for setting themselves up to be abused, for not doing more to escape. This destructive attitude is very prevalent amongst victims of abuse. However, it seems to be a common consequence of many major personal disasters. Victims of other natural disasters often blame themselves for being there, or for not doing more. Bereaved individuals often feel guilty about still being alive or about minor arguments they had with the deceased prior to their death. In all these cases it can cause major problems for the victim if it cannot be resolved, and contributes considerably to their distress.

It is seldom that direct confrontation or reassurance will change attitudes towards self blame. These approaches are too easily rationalized by the client as the therapist making up reasons for not blaming themselves or trying to be nice. A more effective approach involves therapist and client collaborating to examine the evidence which the client is using to justify her self blame. Close examination of victims' reasons for blaming themselves usually demonstrates them to be either unreasonable, 'I shouldn't have been at home on my own, even if the door was locked', or obvious only in hindsight, 'I should have known he wanted more than coffee.' Often, also, victims blame themselves for not doing more to resist or escape. However, at the time, in the circumstances of the abuse, their choices were far more limited than often seems to them to be the case afterwards.

It is important to help them come to an awareness of this in their own way. Often this involves asking them what else they could have done at each stage where their hindsight suggests they were responsible or could have done more, and systematically examining the feasibility of any other options thrown up. In general, most of the other options prove to be illusory. This is particularly so when account is taken of the victim's state of mind at the time of the assault, and the risks involved in resistance. Another way in which this problem can be tackled is to promote free discussion of the issue in small groups of victims. The realization that others found themselves just as helpless in similar situations and, perhaps more importantly, that they also blame themselves can be very effective. Often it is when a victim is trying to help another overcome their particular guilt that they suddenly realize that the arguments apply equally well to themselves. Essentially both these approaches to this problem rely on the same process: the client has to convince themself that they are not guilty, rather than be convinced by others. Relieving the burden of guilt in this way often can be crucial for overcoming, at least in part, the experience of depression, where this is fuelled by self blame.

To be able to be convinced that they are not to blame, many clients have to be taught that they have the right to blame others. Many victims of abuse have considerable difficulty in standing up for their own rights or even accepting that they have rights. It is not uncommon that victims will blame themselves but lay no blame at the door of the abuser. Many find it difficult to get angry at the offender for what they have done, or indeed to express anger of any kind towards anyone. These are all problems of assertion, which can be a major stumbling block for many victims coming to terms with their experiences. Often assertion training, including a full discussion of personal rights, can help. Sometimes this needs to be done before attempting to diminish self blame in the ways described above. Assertion training can be done in a number of ways, both individually and in groups. It involves teaching clients that they have rights and how to assert these rights without trampling over those of others in the process, as this would be aggression. It usually involves looking at more appropriate ways of dealing with situations and finally providing practice to develop confidence in the new skills. It is often particularly relevant to victims of abuse for two reasons. Firstly it can help them express appropriate anger about their experiences and secondly, it can also help them to reduce their vulnerability in the future, a not uncommon problem for victims.

A third, unfortunately common problem associated with abuse seems to be impulses to inflict injury on oneself. At present there has been very little research linking this directly with abuse, but as more and more people are becoming prepared to admit to experiences of abuse, evidence for there being a link between the two is becoming stronger. At present, however, it is not clear whether impulses to self injury are more associated with sexual abuse or physical abuse or equally associated with both. It may be, for example, that only those who have experienced physical abuse, whether or not in the context of sexual abuse, are prone to these impulses. We simply do not know at the present time. It does not follow, however, that everyone who has urges to harm themselves has undergone some experience of sexual or physical abuse.

As well as little research having been done on the causes of self injury, there has also been little research on the possible psychological treatments. It does seem that many people who inflict self harm feel tension building inside them which is only relieved when they injure themselves. The greater the tension, the greater the injury required to relieve it. In a few cases, victims have described a voice which seems to come from inside their head, telling them to harm themselves, or others. People who go through with some form of self harm, for example cutting themselves, often report that they experienced no pain at the time, while others indicate that the pain is necessary to achieve relief from tension.

All these are anecdotal accounts, however, with little systematic research to clarify what is happening.

Urges to self harm fall into the category of what psychologists call compulsive urges. This kind of urge typically gets stronger for a while then gradually fades away if the victim does not give in to it. If the victim does give in to the urge, even partially, by, for example, allowing themselves to fantasize about harming themselves, then they tend to get stronger and more frequent. Like flashbacks they can be triggered by cues which have been associated in some way with the abuse experience and also with previous situations where self harm has actually occurred. This means that the more often a victim can resist these urges, the more likely it is that they will weaken and become less frequent, although this may not be apparent right away. People who have, in the past, given in to urges to self harm may require a lot of support in resisting them to start with. However, the longer they manage to resist, the easier it should get. It is important to remember that even fantasizing about self harm is a way of giving in and will strengthen and prolong the problem.

It is not always possible not to give in to urges to self harm, especially if the person has been giving in to them for a long time, or when they occur frequently and in situations where the therapist cannot easily provide support to resist them initially. Other ways of resisting or replacing these urges have been suggested, but none has been properly tested scientifically, although clinical reports suggest that they can be very effective. One approach is to try to displace aggression onto safe, inanimate objects, for example, a punchbag or pillow, or smashing old crockery. Other approaches have used the creation of *non-harmful* pain, by, for example, exercising past the point of pain; or where the urges are too frequent, perhaps to use less obtrusive methods such as squeezing your fist or a soft rubber ball, or pad tightly *beyond* the point where this causes pain, every time an urge to self injure occurs. Physical exercise has been proved to be beneficial and to lead to a considerable reduction in the frequency of urges to self harm in one therapeutic experiment. Despite the fact that many victims seem to experience no pain at the time of self injury, the deliberate creation of pain may have a similar tension-reducing effect.

Depression can be a prolonged problem after physical and sexual abuse. Psychological research on depression has shown that it is usually associated with poor self opinion, although this is usually unjustified. Once a person is depressed, other quite natural reactions tend to maintain the depression. For example, it has been demonstrated that depressed people tend to become biased about the way they experience and remember events. They become less and less able to recognize positive experiences for what they are, while at the same time they become more prone to interpret their experiences as demonstrating how worthless they are. This tendency is aided and abetted by a memory bias in which they become selectively less able to remember positive events which have happened to them and more able to remember unpleasant events. It becomes more and more difficult to retain a balanced view on life and they become increasingly prone to look on themselves, the world and their future as black and hopeless. The more they think about these things the more depressed they become. It all becomes a vicious circle.

Often, periods of depression are triggered by incidents which remind victims of their experiences of abuse. For example, trigger flashbacks and associated panic reactions or urges to self injure can create periods of depression. Continued uncontrollable flashbacks and panic can continue the feeling of helplessness and so depression goes on. Other sources of feelings of depression in victims of sexual abuse include real fears of vulnerability in the future, inability to accept one's own abused self, coupled with beliefs about never being clean again, and real fears of rejection by others if the abuse becomes known. Unless the particular problems of the individual victim are properly addressed they remain to act as the core of ongoing feelings of depression. Some victims can find themselves still prone to depression many years after the abuse has stopped.

One of the ways in which this vicious circle can be broken is by cognitive behaviour therapy. This is a very complex form of therapy but is becoming more and more available as its effectiveness is demonstrated time and again with depressed people. Put simply, it consists of three stages. Firstly, in order to help people distract themselves from the constant flow of depressive thoughts, it usually starts with prescribing simple activities, especially selected to provide some genuine experience of success. This, in itself, often can help lift depression enough to proceed to the next stage, although by itself, it usually provides only temporary relief. The next stage is to try to find out what it is the person is saying to themselves which is maintaining the low self concept and the depressed mood. This can be much more difficult than it would appear. Very often the responsible thoughts or self-statements are so well practised as to be almost automatic, in fact one author calls them 'automatic thoughts'. These can be difficult to identify, but typically have the characteristic that they are immediately followed by a worsening of the depressed mood. Finally, once these self-statements are clarified, to examine each as objectively as possible, reviewing the evidence for and against them. This is what depressed people are unable to do for themselves. Once they become more able to objectively assess their experiences, they often find little difficulty in rejecting their previous, very biased interpretations, and break the vicious circle which has been responsible for maintaining their depressed mood. In the case of victims of prolonged sexual abuse, much groundwork of the kind described in the preceding sections may be necessary before they become able to view their automatic thoughts objectively.

Drug treatments for depression are very effective these days, and should by no means be rejected out of hand, especially where a victim is severely depressed. Unfortunately they do not take away the fact of abuse or its consequences, so there may be a possibility that those who respond to this type of treatment may become depressed again after the drugs are withdrawn. At the present time it is difficult to tell how likely this would be in victims of abuse. They do, however, often provide early relief. Most take about three to four weeks to work effectively and are not addictive as far as we know at the present time. It may be that the best treatment is to combine drugs with cognitive behaviour therapy so as to obtain the benefits of both types of treatment.

The consequences of sexual abuse discussed in this chapter are by no means universal. Perhaps they only apply to a very small proportion of victims, let us hope so. Many people undergo forms of abuse and survive relatively intact. Some of these have been known to worry why they haven't been affected more by their experiences, and what that might say about them. In fact it says no more than that people are different and react differently and that perhaps their experiences were less traumatic or prolonged or that they had more resources to cope with them than others.

I am acutely aware that in this short review I have been able to only skim the surface of the effects of sexual abuse and their treatment. This is partly because we only understand relatively little about it as yet. There are many other consequences of abuse I have not touched upon. I have tried to describe some of the more serious and to show that ways are being developed to overcome them and, perhaps more importantly, to enable victims themselves to overcome the aftermath. Therapy is often not easy, for therapists as well as victims, but increasingly there is evidence that it is worthwhile and effective. We have a long way to go. We don't know enough to claim to be able to help everyone, or even to completely understand why one victim has one set of symptoms and another a different set. One thing is clear, the more victims who come forward, the faster will we progress and the more will be able to be helped to help themselves. There is hope.

Thanks to Sue Lewis, Clinical Psychologist, for her help in reviewing this chapter.

Afraid to love

Susan, Sarah, David, Sandy and Julie are just some of the thousands of people in Britain today living with the effects of child sexual abuse.

Susan a capable, hard-working teacher who is liked enormously by her colleagues and loved by her pupils, goes home every evening to sit on the stairs, holding her teddy, crying out the emotion she has held in check all day.

Sarah is seen to be a loving, caring mother. Her husband works in a bank and they live in a nice part of town. But behind the closed doors of her home Sarah is petrified of changing her baby Michael's nappy; it makes her feel dirty and ashamed. She cannot sleep with her husband. She is frightened of the dark and of being left alone.

David is obsessively clean. He washes his hands after changing his clothes, sitting down, eating at table, being with people he knows. All the time, this feeling of being dirty pushes him towards water and a cleansing process which makes him feel better only until he touches or brushes past what to him has become the next obstacle in his life.

Sandy is bulimic. To those outside, she maintains an enviable figure which all her friends admire. At home, she crams biscuits, chocolate, sandwiches, pies, and all manner of food into her mouth, gaining a brief respite of comfort to ward off the rigours of the day, giving way to the feelings of desperation and loneliness she tries so hard to hide. Then, pushing her fingers down her throat, she makes herself sick, punishing herself for the kind of person she feels she has become.

Julie is a talented writer. She is a success in all she does. But most evenings she spends punishing herself, burning herself with cigarettes, cutting her legs. If she digs deep enough she hopes to cut out all the poison she feels she was given in her sexually abusive past. She doesn't believe that she deserves her success. She sees herself as a freak, a failure, incapable of love, or of leading a normal adult life. This is the legacy left to her by her abuser.

The terrible thing about living in the aftermath of sexual abuse is that, for most of the time, its effects cannot be seen. While outwardly the victim effects several layers of copeability, inwardly she remains a seething mass of emotion, anguish and fear. She protects herself fiercely from further hurt and harm. Once betrayed, she no longer knows who to trust. Anyway, who is going to believe that this apparently capable, hard-working person still has horrendous problems to overcome unless she has an emotional blowout and is found wandering in her nightdress or violently threatening unknown forces with a knife.

In the same way as a camera freezes an emotive moment, the mind is capable of holding a frozen fragment of fear, distorted through our vision by terror and dread. Physically, the abused may be able to move on. Outwardly they are seen to adapt to a new way of life. They re-adjust themselves to take on board the new dent to their confidence and self-esteem. They believe they have lived through and coped with their fear and the trauma that, for a spell, interrupted their flow. Many of them do not even remember, anaesthetized as they are against the pain.

What can only become apparent in the future is that the incubated fear is still a part of them, a part of their make-up, ruling the way in which they live their future lives. In the end, it cannot be forgotten or denied. Just as we automatically put a hand up to save ourselves if threatened, past experience transmits a learned response, so that at any time, a trigger is capable of setting off that same fear, that same desperation and dread the victim felt during the time of their experience. Then those incubated feelings are reawakened, and they feel over again the pain of the moment, swamping them in a massive pit of depression and gloom where we lose the point to it all.

Jane has been recovering from a series of operations, stemming from a complicated hysterectomy. While she was recovering, she happened to catch sight of a broom left leaning against the door, an ordinary, everyday utensil in most households. Her immediate response was one of fear. Within seconds, she was in shock, drenched in sweat, shaking, crying, her churning stomach making her feel very sick.

Only later, when she was calmer, did she bravely confront her pattern of behaviour, attempting to trace it to source. That broom in fact triggered an image from her past, replaying back the film in her mind of the moment her ex-husband had snatched up a similar long-handled broom to use as an instrument of rape.

For Jane, a broom triggers a conditioned response, and her learned pattern of behaviour is displayed in the fear which comes after.

So many survivors today say to me, 'If only we could take out our experience and hand it over for a while to our carers, to those who just don't know, so that they might feel our pain, recognize our shame, our abuse, and help them to understand what we cannot fully put into words.' Sometimes words are not enough. Emotion isn't always something that can be expressed, except by getting angry, by crying, by feeling what we want to say inside. When the abused cannot fully put their experiences across to the concerned professional sitting on the other side of the desk with only a limited amount of time to spare, they become confused, distressed, and end up carrying their bottle of pills home, diagnosed as a depressive, a hypochondriac, a hysterical, fantasizing manic mess. They become one of the misunderstood.

As time goes on, they become guilty of wasting people's time, of not being able to cope, unable to put their past behind them and to get on with their lives.

Another part of their guilt is fed by the belief that they are contaminating their family because they, in turn, become a part of the problem. Those who were not with the abused at the time of their experience cannot appreciate how much their past lives are a part of their today. They cannot fully know or understand, however much they would wish, however much they try. Those who are sufficiently supportive take on the burden, attempting

to find ways to help us through. The abused still feel contami-
nated, and feel that they are carrying on the cycle by contaminating
through contact those they love.

So the victims turn their anger and hate inwards. They feel they
deserve to be punished, because of their present feelings and the
effects on their families today. They believe it is their duty to continue the pattern of punishment themselves which began when
they were first abused. Without the chance of re-education to break
the pattern they have accepted since their experience, they can
become like Rachael, who stabs herself repeatedly in the stomach,
or Bobbie who cuts and burns her body, which she has grown
to hate.

One of the most difficult emotions to come to terms with from
the past is that of guilt, and it is often hard to push it firmly back
with the abuser where it belongs. It may seem black and white
to outsiders, but those who have lived the experience are conditioned to expect punishment as a part of their lives. The abused
feel guilty, feel that they are to blame. It is because they deserve
to be punished that they feel their future lives are going to be
such a mess.

Every victim needs to learn how to move on to become a survivor and to accept what happened. They need to place the guilt
firmly back with the abuser where it belongs, and to begin to
believe in themselves.

Therapy is a vital part of a survivor's recovery. They have to
have that place where they can go. They need that special someone with whom to confront their fears, to remember, and to learn
to let the past go.

Different things work for different people, and it became important to find what was right for me. When I first met Mike, my
second husband, now ten years ago, I remembered little about
my past. I had blotted what I could not cope with from my mind
inadvertently anaesthetizing myself against the pain of remembered abuse. Mistakenly, I believed that because I could not remember, I had therefore dealt with the traumas of my life, and was
once more 'better', once more a whole and complete person.

People would say how lucky I was at having found my 'happy
ever-after' ending, and even after writing my first book, I believed
I had put my past ghosts to rest. With a supportive husband, a
nice house, and the child I was told I could never have, every

thing had fitted beautifully into place. So why then was I feeling a churning in my stomach? Why did I suffer from migraines when there was no stress? Why did my hands shake, my vision blur, and my whole being become tired and depressed for no reason?

It was easy at first to put it down to the general strain of living, of having deadlines to meet, and a busy schedule to fulfil. After the birth of my baby, these feelings began to escalate, and at times I felt completely out of control. In fact, far from confronting my fears and working them back to source, I had pushed them down, boxing them away in the farthest corners of my mind. Now they were letting me know they were there, leaking emotion, pushing forward to interfere with my life today.

The right kind of therapy does not always immediately come to hand, as I was to find to my cost. Sometimes those in the medical profession have to be convinced that what the abused say is true, that the effects of the past are as horrific as they say. The story of abuse which victims carry with them often goes beyond another's normality, so it is then easy for others to dismiss it as a work of fiction. When the abused do not immediately fit into a textbook ailment the professionals become confused about what to do for the best, questioning experiences and putting forward the theory that it is nothing more than a dream. Meanwhile, the victim is further injured by the rejection, and reaches that point when they begin to wonder themselves if they are in fact going mad.

I found myself having to fight off prescriptions for tranquillizers and anti-depressants. Pills weren't going to solve my problem; they couldn't deal with my problem at source. Besides, I'd already tried it. In the past, I'd taken pills to relieve the agony of being a battered wife. They weren't the answer for me, and so I kept hammering away, looking for therapy that felt right for me, that dealt with my symptoms at source. I refused to accept second best, or to be pushed into a more convenient treatment which just wasn't for me.

For ten weeks I saw a psychoanalyst, who saw me for exactly an hour. For the entire session there could be total silence unless I talked. I wasn't encouraged, and I didn't feel I was getting anything back from my sharing, or making sense of what I said. I didn't feel able to switch myself on and off at will like a machine. In fact, my feelings carried on long after I had returned home, and I was left with emotions for which I had no ready means of coping on my own. I had not been taught how. The psychoanalytical approach might work for some people, but it didn't suit me.

For a while after that, Mike and I saw a sex therapist, using the Masters and Johnson technique for overcoming fear of sex. Beginning with touching and holding hands and a total ban on intercourse, we found out what we each enjoyed, learning about giving and accepting without fear of being out of control. And yet, more and more, as we tried the exercises in our own home, we found my problems reached further back. Images from my past locked into place, and Mike got mixed up with my abuser. I cowered back, feeling abused, my imagery preventing me from moving on. Still we had not reached the source.

Our doctor at the time asked me to talk to a psychiatrist, who could see nothing wrong with me. She offered me a place to talk if I ever felt the need, and left it at that, and then again, there were always the pills. Rather like being a battered woman and showing outward scars as a visible sign of distress, she needed me to externalize my problems, to bring out the kind of feelings I felt so bad about inside. Again, I didn't know how. Such a turmoil of emotion churned around in the pit of my stomach that it would have been like following a single thread through a maze of wool.

Finally, a new doctor entered our local practice. He referred me to a clinical psychologist, and for the first time I felt I had found someone who listened to my needs instead of trying to fit me into a pigeonhole ailment for which there was a textbook cure. He was willing to learn to understand my problem enough to teach me how to deal with it at source.

Everyone who has ever suffered sexual abuse will carry around with him or her some aspect of the past which they fear. Each victim will have images of his or her experiences and these become magnified. It was those images, I recognized, which were feeding my nightmares, my fits of depression, the feelings of guilt and shame, inadequacy and despair, and all those hundreds of feelings which had been building up inside me from the first moment I needed help, and even before. For me, the greatest hurt was the rape. I had moved on from a battered wife to a survivor of sexual abuse.

At first, working with my therapist, I thought I would find a overall formula which would work, something to take away my bad feelings and make me whole. But then as I began to talk about and accept my past, I realized that the kind of person I had become was dependent on my experiences then. It wasn't all just going to fall back into place. I wasn't going to regain my confidence, my self-respect and be able to make my marriage work just like that. My experience had changed me; it had given me a new perception of myself, a different kind of normality with which I had to learn to cope. In the end, I could never dump my past, nor could I change it or ignore it. It wasn't ever going to go away, but I could learn to live with what I had, to cope, to survive, to understand myself and to like myself and be happy with myself and what I had become.

Drawing a map of myself helped me to externalize those feelings I felt within (see Fig. 2).

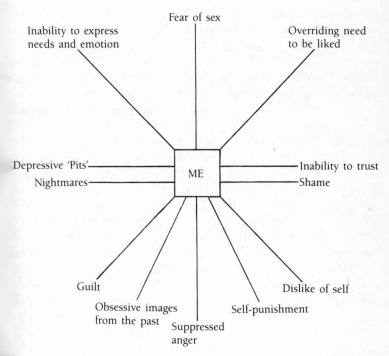

Fig. 2

In fact, finding out about ourselves is an important part of the process of moving from being a victim to a survivor of sexual abuse. Compiling a spider graph such as the one illustrated in Fig. 2 is an excellent way to begin. It is a way to externalize feelings and, once drawn, it enabled me to share with my counsellor in a way he could understand.

The next step is to talk the various points through, to understand the past incidents which have influenced the abused. This matching process is again helpful in building up a jigsaw of what has gone before.

My own therapy became a learning process for my therapist as well as for myself. He allowed me to talk out my past, homing in on each of the compass points on my map of self, encouraging me through my fear, pushing a path through the confusion which was producing such a tight knot of feeling within.

As I relived my experiences, I realized more and more that I became depressed whenever another door opened and memory was restored. It was a way of telling me there was more to come and that I was going to have to readjust myself and prepare to accept another incident of hurt.

During these low periods — what I called 'Pits' — I had nightmares and suffered panic attacks. I became bulimic, binging on chocolate and ice-cream. There were days when I couldn't allow myself to be touched or to have anyone standing near me. I wanted to shut myself away from the real world, to hide what I had become. I felt dirty, frigid, freaky and I began to lose the point of it all.

This form of manic depression made each day feel as if I was climbing an endless mountain. Each hour ticked by monotonously, however busy I tried to become. Everything became an effort. I was lethargic, listless, on edge. I had a car accident when an obsessive image from my past splurged across the windscreen. I didn't see the juggernaut coming towards me on the narrow bridge until it was too late. During another period of depression, I fainted in the bath after recalling that first moment of rape by the canal.

'The Pits', as I named them, can be likened to a child's dot-to-dot drawings where each dot is an oasis, a relief from the depression in between. It is important for everyone to find something which works for them, some way to pull them through. I mapped out a dot-to-dot chart of recovery in preparation for the times when I would go into a new 'Pit'.

Monday
Spend day in town
calling at library

Sunday
Pamper Day —
when I do
something for
myself

Tuesday
Attend sexual abuse
survivors self-help
group

Eat regularly.
Get out once a day.
Meet someone to talk to.
Find somewhere which feels
safe to go to when bad.

Saturday
Stay with family
or friend or take
family out for day

Wednesday
Springclean
house

Friday
Write letters,
begin a project,
start a study of
something I have always
been interested in
but never had incentive
or time

Thursday
Involve myself in an
activity outside the
home to maintain
outside contact —
sports club, swimming,
yoga, jogging, meditation,
drama, self-defence.
Any activity I would not
usually do

Each oasis gave me something to aim for, some point of contact with the outside world. I needed to know I was not alone, that there was someone there for me.

Outside 'the Pits', I could cope. In fact, I felt a tremendous sense of achievement and well-being. It put me on a high to know that I was actually coming out of 'the Pits' knowing more about myself than before. At last I was learning to break free from the chains of my past. Early on I decided that out of every negative there had to come a positive, something that could work for me in the future.

Realizing that externalizing my feelings in the beginning on my spider graph had moved me a step further on, I urged myself to keep a diary of emotion while I remained depressed, looking for some good to come out of all that bad.

Having moments when I sat and thought about how I felt, then writing those feelings down, was enough to help. The diary showed my step-by-step progression of change. Routine was important, as a working plan for the day gave me oases to aim for through the depression that otherwise was in danger of taking over my life.

Here are some extracts from my diary:

Thursday

A picture of the past is with me and it will not let me go. I have an awful sense of *it* being in control rather than me. For the rest of the day, it lies like a scar on my soul, sickeningly real, conjuring up other images while I frantically try to stuff them back where they belong.

My stomach somersaults, leaving a residue of fear and foreboding. A feeling of unreality traps me behind glass. I am worthless, I am dirty, I am frigid, I am poisoned, passing venom like a disease on to everyone I meet. I see myself in the reflection of a window; I am a stranger. She isn't the person I see within, but façade, displayed for the world.

I sit in the car trembling, agitated, panic-stricken. My head aches and the black Pit swallows me up into a well of despair with terrible familiarity and pain.

Friday

Hurting like hell! I never knew it could be so bad. I've got diarrhoea, stomach cramps, fits of uncontrollable shaking; I've no interest in food (very unusual!), tension in my neck and head and I cry almost all the time. It is like driving a car whose headlights are picking out those parts of my past that I fear most, that even now continue to hurt and to shame, oblivious of all else. I feel all the symptoms above in a constant state of helplessness, totally unable to cope internally with everyday life. My image no longer needs a trigger, something that will bring it into play. I can no longer switch it on and off, now I suffer a perpetual state of hurting. One day merges into another. The image which was once a side issue has now taken over my life.

I think I'm having some kind of breakdown.

Saturday

It still hurts like hell. I have tremendous problems even finding where the image first starts before I am completely over-whelmed with a massive panic attack. I am now talking daily with my therapist, together with a fellow sufferer I have found. Sharing helps me to know I am not alone. Someone understands and knows because he has been there before me. He has that X-factor of experience similar to my own.

Sunday

Yesterday I couldn't do anything but feel, my thoughts were numbed. That all-pervading ache pulsated through my body. I work today to pictures of the past which mix with reality. My abuser is there, on the bus, across the street, walking towards me. He is always there, wherever I am or I will be. The wall of the shop is the same as the factory wall across the canal where I was raped. I can hear the sound of water, and footsteps, and I see a figure. I am afraid, my stomach churns and I feel sick. I want to run away, but it's only the town centre on a Saturday. Bodies press around me, they are suffocatingly close, and I feel stifled. I have to get away.

Tuesday

Nightmares. I wake up sweating in the night. A dark shape stands over me by the side of my bed — the silent watcher. For an eternity, I shake. I panic, already feeling a red hot poker searing up my insides. The *pain*. I am crying. He is there. I know what he will do.

My hand reaches for the light, fighting between past and present. There is no one there. I am alone.

Nightmares — I am running away into a tunnel of black-ness. It becomes a giant wave washing over me, swamping, suffocating, squeezing the breath from my body. Gasping, I wake, soaked in sweat. Headachy, sick, tired, but unwilling to sleep because of my fear of the beyond and the terrors that lurk in the night.

Wednesday

The extraordinary days I can cope with. It's the ordinary days I can't cope with. They become my OD days, the days when I feel swamped by emotion of the past. I become a child, abused, betrayed. I feel hurt, rejected, frightened, alone. Who is here for me? Where can I hide away from the pain?

Is it that I can cope with the extraordinary days because I have been programmed to deal with them in my past? Sitting on a time bomb, wondering when he would explode, left me with a normality of perpetual near-excitement, near-boiling. It tears my nerves to shreds, but it's something I've been programmed for. I feel it's where I belong, yet I have to break free.

Friday

There are many moments in my life like now when I am caught in a tangled knot of feeling that will not let me go. I struggle, terrified, screaming quietly inside where no one will hear. The bonds of the past hold me, suffocating, squeezing away whatever life there was left to look forward to in the future.

Images flit across my world, slipping between me and reality, causing an illusion of a part-wakeful dream. Like a hand held up, fingers spread in front of a face, the image is there, tangible, solid, reality for me rather than illusion. It draws me in, suddenly and violently catapulting me back through time to a past I want so desperately to forget.

There, back once more in that room, where the purple curtains sway gently in the breeze, the walls close in, securing me in a vice that will not let me go. Fingers touch and hold. An ache creeps slowly like a shiver up the back of my spine, down through my body. Sweat breaks out of my pores, soaking me in memories, holding them within as a sponge holds water. And as I squeeze through that first initial shock, my mind refills, emptying and filling, filling and emptying, until the nightmare is complete.

I feel cold, isolated, and insecure. I am once more my shadow, following the rhythm and beat of the music I know well. I turn the page of the well-read book and feel the ache spread. It churns within, reaching all parts of my body, eating up the good and leaving only bad.

I have no rights because I am no longer worthy. This is me, the me I know so well. It was wrong to hide and it is wrong to cry; the punishment is mine.

Like a frightened child, I gaze with widened eyes at the

creature I have become. I am ashamed of the person that is me. I feel guilty about what I have allowed to happen. I have been violated as a woman. I feel humiliated, embarrassed, ashamed, confused.

My husband, what am I doing to you? You don't deserve this. Why do you stay with this part-woman, part-child? And how can I tell you all that I was made to do?

Isolated. Alone. Yearning for something which can never be. I struggle through my thoughts, screwed up tight with remembered pain. They say the image can no longer hurt, but how do they know? How can they say this when I cry out with the pain of what that image does?

This is me. The person I never want you to know. Shame, guilt, despair draw me down, away from this life to which I have no right. Where am I going? Who will I be? Who will love and like and care? Where am I going? Who will I be? Who will love and care? Mike, you have given so much. And I have denied you. You deserve more. You deserve a life which will offer richness and quality. Dredged in memory, I can only ever bring you down.

Somehow, when you arrive home tonight, I must be here, waiting, the welcoming wife. As I write these words, I am freeing a part of myself, letting it go. I feel the relief. When you come, I shall be here.

By the end of this 'Pit' I was beginning to feel that something good might come of it. Out of 'the Pit' came the positive knowledge that I did have some guidelines which I could follow during subsequent depressions in the future. They couldn't take away the confusion of feeling inside, but they could at least give me a means of coping with what I had, offering a positive out of the negative which had gone before.

Panic attacks

Because I had kept a diary I was able to pinpoint the times when I was most vulnerable to panic attacks, and to work out how to cope with them. The attacks are most likely to occur:

- When I have to get up to face a new day. Most of all, I dread weekends when there is no absolute routine I must follow to keep me going, to give me something to aim at, someone to meet

● When my daughter wakes in the night, pulling me out of sleep to face the stark reality of life once more, realizing as I do that I have been living a nightmare of the past. I am afraid then to go back to sleep, to return to my dreams

● When I am asked by anyone about how I am feeling and why. Too many people live in the mistaken belief that a door can be shut on the past, allowing us to get on with our life

● When confronted by a man resembling my abuser

● When having to cope with responsibilities of running house and home with a husband who works away most of the time

● When I see a stubbed-out cigarette in an ashtray it reminds me vividly of the times when I was abused with cigarettes

● When I see a man rolling cigarette papers and tobacco. My ex-husband used to do the same, always menacingly, before the punishment which was to come.

●After talking with Mike, especially at night on the phone, trying to explain indescribable feelings

● When I am alone at home for any long period of time with no one to talk to but my baby.

Symptoms of a panic attack

● Quick short breaths, often catching in the throat

● A churning of the stomach

● Shaking and trembling

● Inability to concentrate on anything other than problem

● Tension across shoulders causing a tight band across head, leading to headaches/migraines

● Eating irrationally — either too little or too much

● Nausea

- Feelings of being on the outside looking in

- Helpless feelings of being unable to cope

- Hot flushes, sweating, or shivering and coldness

- Insomnia

- Diarrhoea.

A personal means of coping with attacks

- Take a deep breath, hold it, and then let it out slowly, saying to yourself, 'Calm... calm... calm'

- Concentrate on your breathing and try to slow it down. Aim to find what triggers off a panic attack. Learn to anticipate one by recognizing symptoms before they reach a peak. Get it under control rather than letting *it* control *you*

- Have a set time each day for yourself. Learn to relax. Concentrate on tensing and relaxing each muscle in your body in turn. Always be aware of the pace of your breathing

- If your breathing does get out of control, and you find yourself breathing too fast, breathe into a paper bag, holding it securely over your nose and mouth. Breathe in and out, in and out slowly, until the breathing finally slows down.

- If the attacks get too bad and you feel you really cannot continue, then it is advisable to visit your doctor. Your GP may be able to prescribe something for you to take temporarily which will help to calm you until you feel able to cope on your own.

- Try to keep a diary, noting what triggers off an attack and also your feelings at that time. This can help the doctor or therapist decide what is best for you.

Therapy

At further sessions my therapist and I agreed that what needed to be confronted before going further was the over-riding image which pushed me into 'the Pit'. We set aside a day for dealing with the image which came as a result of a particular fear from my past.

It was a frightening experience. In the beginning it was easier to push that image away, to think of something else, anything that readily came to mind, blocking out that fear with which I could not cope. I cried with remembered emotion. It felt okay to cry because I was with someone who believed, who understood, who felt safe to be with, and who shared that experience with me in that room. I felt that experience with me in that room. I felt humiliated and ashamed as I allowed myself to be raped again in memory, to cast myself back in order once more to be punished and abused. I had to feel once more the pain and an overwhelming burning sensation within to be able to see it as it really was.

My therapist and I worked together for four hours, rating my progress on a scale between 1 and 10. I had anxiety and panic attacks and I was reduced to a shivering, shaking wreck. In time these feelings receded, giving way to a growing sense of calm which strengthened and grew even as I once more forced myself to face the picture of my past which had become that image of today. With that image, I began to feel less devastated, less afraid.

The following day marked the end of another 'Pit', and I wrote in my diary.

Sunday
Today I feel I have made a tremendous leap forward. I can live with myself. I like myself. All things are possible.

Working through another 'Pit', I went on a monastic retreat

for two weeks, feeling I needed to be by myself. It was like going on a long journey of self discovery. I returned with a deeper and more positive insight into the working of my mind, and my conditioned responses to today. Looking back, I felt that enormous sense of satisfaction and relief in realizing I had moved on.

Monday

I am more assertive with Mike, testing out new responses with the guidance of a book I borrowed from my therapist entitled *When I Say No I Feel Guilty.* Mike is already remarking on a different, more positive me.

My inner ache is gone. The image is dispelled for the time being. I feel a deep new inner sense of peace. I am introducing past interests back into my life, realizing that I shut them off when I first met Mike. Because my past relationship was wrong, I somehow came to believe that everything about that time was wrong. I went in search of a new me, a me without the trappings of the past, trying to shut the door on those experiences that had wounded and hurt. I have always asked and been given Mike's approval in everything I do today, the clothes I wear, my music, my writing. I feel I have needed that. Any negative response on his part I have interpreted as rejection, and I have therefore rejected that task, believing it to be wrong.

Now, in my newly adopted role, I have re-introduced into my life my own kind of beliefs. I write songs, but in my style rather than in his; I read escapist books to replace those Mike thought I should read; I write what I want to write and not what I feel is expected of me, I experiment with make-up; I think irrational thoughts without needing to justify them; I go out socially regardless of whether or not I will have Mike as a partner; I buy Christmas and birthday presents that I want to buy which Mike will consider trivial.

I feel altogether a very much more fulfilled, complete and positive person, as if I have somehow uncovered a part of myself. I have hidden for so long.

later 'Pits' I discovered that, as I learned to cope with my pictures from the past, my first obsessive image was replaced by another. I coped with that, but in turn there was yet another and another until I became frightened that I was in a spriralling circle of abuse in which there was no beginning or end. One memory was prompting the next.

Writing wasn't enough. It could no longer describe what I was seeing in my mind's eye. I needed to find a way to bring it out, to once more externalize not only the emotion, but the picture as a whole. No one else could do this for me. Only I saw it as it was for me.

Fear distorts. An abuser becomes larger than life, the god of all evil. A bedroom where abuse took place becomes a prison, closing in on all sides. One day, I found the courage to sit down and draw what I saw in the way it happened to me. First I found it easier to do it in the third person, as if I were looking in on a scene, but the way which worked and best illustrated my past was drawing from my view. My view on the grass during rape, my view in the bedroom from the bed and in the kitchen; wherever the abuse had taken place. Alongside these scenes, I found it worked for me to draw pictures of feelings which I could not yet find a way of putting into words. Two examples of those pictures are on pp. 163 and 164.

Finally, through experience, by writing and drawing and sharing with fellow survivors like myself, I found a formula to illustrate what happens in the aftermath of sexual abuse.

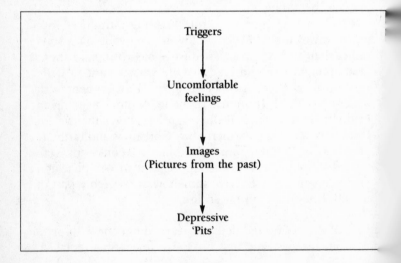

Examples of the drawings in which I expressed the feelings that could not be put into words. The door into the bedroom (*this page*) and the abuser (*overleaf*).

Everyone has to find their trigger points: those times in their life which remind them of an abusive past. Writing and drawing my way through 'the Pits', I found my own triggers. Listing them gave me the ability to recognize when I was most at risk of falling prey to depressive feelings of guilt, shame and despair.

Triggers

- Letting go
- Getting angry
- Feeling rejected
- Guilt
- Stress
- Feeling hurt and/or afraid
- Being abused
- Having an argument

- Someone holding something in a threatening way

- Untidiness

- Autumn tree

- Water

- Stubbing out cigarettes

- The dark

- Deep purple (that was the colour of the curtains in the room where I was most abused)

- Having sex

- Saying 'No'

- Closeness/holding/hugging by Mike or family

- Something personal getting broken

- Periods

- Going to the dentist because of how he stands over me

- A hand in front of my face.

Uncomfortable feelings

- Stomach churning

- Headachy/migraine

- Feeling dizzy

- Shaking

- Hyperventilating (breathing too frequently)

- Twitching, jumpiness

- Disorientation

- Helplessness.

Images

These vary according to the trigger and the image of violence and rape it conjures from past.

Depressive 'Pits'

These are characterized by:

- Nightmares
- Insomnia
- Food disorders
- Constantly crying
- Tension
- Confused state
- Lack of concentration
- Listlessness
- Fatigue
- Feelings of pointlessness
- Self-punishment
- Feeling dirty
- Feeling ashamed
- Constant thirst
- Turning in on self
- Feelings of living in past
- Aching well of sadness
- Panic attacks
- Sweating or cold and shivering
- Fear

- Irrational thoughts

- Dislike of self

- A feeling of living behind glass

- Faintness/passing out

- Nausea

- Diarrhoea.

Depressive 'Pits' for survivors of sexual abuse can become a way of life. I know people who are still suffering perpetual 'Pits', without the relief of oases inbetween. They live from one hour to the next in constant fear, controlled by the images of the past which invade their minds. Everything they see today triggers off a memory they would rather forget, distorted as it is by the abuse and fear they experienced in the past. There is no present and no future in their own minds; they have resigned themselves to living in the past, reliving their abuse over and over and over again. They have not yet found what works for them, or the kind of therapy which can help them to understand and cope, to accept, to believe and to enable them to move on.

Today, I can cope with my 'Pits'. I have confronted my fear of the past and made it work *for* me instead of *against* me, using it in my work. Last year, I took up Ju-Jitsu, realizing that I needed to know what to do if ever faced with a rape situation again. I accepted it as a challenge and, to my surprise, I still find I enjoy my sessions of self-defence. They give me so much more than a means of defending myself against attack and abuse, offering me confidence, raising my self-esteem, allowing me to vent my anger through the movement of the practice sequences.

Over the months I have been doing Ju-Jitsu, I have taken up Shiatsu and meditation as means of relaxation, of looking inward so that I can know and understand myself better. They work for me. They offer me body contact and control, a means of coping with my feelings and they help me develop skills I can use for myself.

In the past, I was trained to be a victim. Unconsciously, I absorbed that learning pattern and adopted it as a part of my every-day life. We remain victims only as long as we accept that role.

We *can* move on, and we *can* break free. By confronting our fear, our anger, our guilt, our shame, we can accept it and reject it, learning to deal with it at source so that we can let it go, allowing ourselves the freedom to laugh, to cry, and to enjoy the true spirit of life. With the right kind of help, we can re-educate ourselves, learn how to turn the negative into the positive, overcome the helplessness we were taught. If we didn't get help as children, we can get it now as adults.

So much depends on how we live with our experiences of the past. We cannot even begin to have the chance of moving on unless we can find someone whom we can trust, who is willing to listen, to understand, to believe, and who is patient enough to learn exactly what our experiences were all about.

I share my past experiences openly and without shame, and I hope I have offered help to those who can identify. Through words, I hope to reach out to other survivors, to let them know they are not alone. There is hope. There is a way of accepting the past, of making it work *for* us instead of *against* us, helping some good come out of all that bad. Survivors of abuse also hope that, through the sharing of their experiences, they may alter people's attitudes to sexual abuse.

Update

Dee
Dee is today using experiences of her past to help others like herself, helping some good come out of all that bad. She has written about what happened to her as a child, when she was abused by her grandfather, and her manuscript entitled, *A Long, Silent Scream* she hopes will one day be published as a book. Dee is also actively involved in the *Bristol Crisis Service for Women,* which focuses on women who may harm themselves as a way of expressing their distress.

Tina
Tina is today living in an impossible situation. She takes one day at a time in the only way she knows how. She lives with her mother, who still cannot come to terms with what has happened to her family, and arguments are rife. Over the coming months, her father is expected out on parole and hopes to return home. Her sister will be getting married and wants nothing more to do with her dad.

While Tina herself feels closest to her father, despite his past abuse of her, they still have to talk about the past and ask those questions which must be uppermost in their minds. Until that sharing of experience and pain, she clings to the hope that one day they will be able to live together as family. She doubts if that can happen. Too many memories stand in the way.

In the meantime, she belongs to a self-help group, but is unsure about what happens after the sharing. She is actively seeking the kind of therapy that feels right for her and is looking for a way to unburden her past.

Mary
Mary is driven by a need to prosecute her father for his abuse

to her as a child. Because she was made to feel guilty for so long, she wants him to realize the long-term effects he caused, and understand that what he did was a crime. Sadly, time may already have run out. It is some years ago since the abuse stopped, but she continues to build up a dossier of events, calling on people who knew her in her past to add their voice to her own.

Sue

Sue now has two children, and in an effort to move herself out of her squat and offer a better life to her daughters, she moved in with her boyfriend Al. Today, she and her family are living in a council house. Sadly, her partner abuses her and she finds her-self once more caught in a trap.

Jane

Jane is desperately trying to find a way of coping with the obses-sive images she carries around from her abusive past. Her doctor has offered her pills to offset the deep depressions she now finds herself in. She and her loving husband are unable to have sex. They have no children.

Gus

Gus hopes he may get parole this year, which will mean he has served nine months of his sentence.

Jerry

Jerry has served six years and still has another nine years of his sentence to go.

Martin

Today Martin has a good job. He still finds relationships difficult and continues to visit his girlfriend at the hospital where she has voluntarily put herself in care. They remain uncertain about their future together.

Directory of advisory services in the UK

Different things work for different people, and it is important, whether you are a victim or a survivor today, to find the kind of ongoing help and support which feels right for you. Our past becomes a part of us which cannot be denied.

This directory has been compiled with the help of the various agencies concerned, in an attempt to take away the suspicion and fear which comes in that first important step of talking to someone about the problem which has become so much a part of you and your life. So many people feel that, in approaching organizations for help, they are putting something into motion which is quickly taken out of their control. We have therefore tried to outline exactly what happens, from the first point of contact with a carer, through to recovery.

The important thing to remember is not to take what is first offered as the only course for you. Find out first what is available. And if something doesn't feel right, you don't have to accept second best. Move on to find something else, something which you feel will perhaps tackle your problem in a way that is right for you.

Learn to talk about your problem. It is only through sharing your feelings that you are going to find the kind of help you need. Otherwise you are being your own worst enemy. Sharing the emotion on its own isn't enough. Feelings are important, but they don't clarify exactly what has happened to you and what it is you need to cope with in the future. It may help to write your experience down in a way a carer can immediately relate to and understand instead of having to deal with what they see as an outward image of breakdown and depression.

Try to deal with the source. Peel away the layers of symptoms in order to find where the root cause of your unhappiness lies.

Help yourself to a better, happier way of life. No one can do this for you. You have to learn to help yourself.

I would be very happy to hear from anyone who has tried the various avenues of help open to them and feels they are not getting the right kind of help, or if the help offered did not turn out as they expected from having read the directory. You can contact me at:

Lifeline
PO Box 251
Marlborough
Wiltshire SN8 1EA

National networks

British Association for Counselling
37a Sheep Street
Rugby
Warwickshire CV21 3BX

Childline
Childline
Freepost 1111
London EC4B 4BB Tel: 0800-1111

This is a free national helpline for children in trouble or danger. Childline offers a confidential counselling service for any child with any problem.

Childline was launched on October 30, 1986 on the *Childwatch* programme on BBC television. The simple, memorable telephone number — 0800 1111 — reached children all over the country.

Children ringing Childline about sexual abuse express many negative feelings which often include fear, humiliation, shame, helplessness and worthlessness. The victim's view of the adult world may have also led him or her to an understanding that it is safest not to invest trust in adults.

Children or young people can be further handicapped by direct pressure from the abuser or indirect pressure from the acquired belief that the activities that they have been involved in are 'bad'.

These pressures combine to provide child victims with the certain knowledge that they hold responsibility for the abuse and further endorse poor self-images and feelings of despair.

One of the strengths of the telephone service offered by Childline lies in its ability to offer children the opportunity to regain some of the power taken from them. The anonymity offered by a telephone conversation has obvious attractions to children attempting to disclose sexual abuse. Equally positive in Childline's experience is the opportunity for each child to end the call at any time. The power is in the child's hands, and replacing the receiver gives a child, perhaps for the first time in years, a measure of control in his or her life.

Childline offers two further positives — confidentiality and truth.

Truth is absolute — there is no exception. Every child who chooses to contact Childline will be given an honest response. The most painful and difficult example of such a policy can be recognized in the following example.

A 12-year-old girl telephones and discloses that she has been sexually abused by her father for a period of two years. She wants the abuse to stop but she does not want to be taken into care, does not want to be involved in court proceedings, does not want her father imprisoned and does not want the family to be fragmented. She has a younger sister whom she is also anxious to protect.

Childline believes that it would be a betrayal and further abuse of the child to offer her anything other than an honest picture. The caller would, therefore, be advised that it could be possible that none of her fears would become reality, but it is also possible that some or indeed all could occur if the abuse were to be disclosed to a statutory agency.

All the possible options are explored with the child as well as any negative or positive thoughts, feelings or emotions involved in pursuing any proffered course of action.

There is only one exception to Childline's strict rule of confidentiality. This arises if the child is perceived to be in a life-threatening situation. Even in such an extreme case, the caller would be advised of Childline's intention to break confidence and the reasons for doing so.

The experience gained by this relatively new agency indicates that callers have considerable difficulty in placing trust in adults.

This is displayed in a number of ways:

- *The silent caller* The child who cannot speak, who needs unhurried encouragement to talk and an acknowledgement that it is difficult to share painful experiences with a stranger.

- *The testing caller* Some callers 'test' counsellors by presenting a substitute problem, by phoning on behalf of a 'friend' or by talking in vague terms about 'not feeling good'. Such children are given time and permission to talk about what is really worrying them or, if this is too difficult, to call back at any time.

- *The return caller* Both silent and testing callers tend to fall into this category. The service offered by Childline allows children to call a number of times until they feel able to share their fears, concerns and anxieties.

The aim of Childline is to allow the troubled and hurt child to speak. By listening and taking them seriously the counsellor can help a child to gain strength, self-respect, and courage — and can help them to be safe.

Childline also receives calls from adults. Over 500 rang in Childline's first year, many about the sexual abuse they had suffered as children. For most people it was the first time they had ever talked to anyone about their suffering. Childline was able to talk to them and refer them to self-help groups and agencies responding specifically to adult victims.

The anguish of these callers, particularly those who have suffered sexual abuse, is so great that many relive their past experiences, presenting themselves to the counsellors as children. With counselling, some of them, trapped in the abuse of the past, are freed and feel able to seek help and support from other agencies.

Other adults call Childline concerned about children who they feel to be in danger, looking for advice about what they can do to protect them. They are referred to the statutory agencies often with the counsellor talking to the agencies first.

Childline also receives calls from abusers wanting to know where to find help and advice to stop their own abusing behaviour. Resources for help, however, are limited. Obviously Childline can not guarantee confidentiality for abusers who call.

(The information on Childline was written by a member of the Childline team.

Childwatch
Dianne Core
60 Beck Road
Everthorpe
North Humberside HU15 2JJ Tel: 04302 3824

Dianne Core, founder of Childwatch (not the BBC Childwatch as mentioned in Childline), was herself a victim of sexual, physical and verbal abuse from her father. She is a committed worker and, since 1985, has been running this nationwide charity from her own home with a team of equally willing and committed helpers. She confronts the issues surrounding child abuse in a direct and effective manner, her primary concern always being the children.

> When people phone, I believe they want a forthright approach to their situation. I will refer all incest survivors for counselling to outside agencies such as Incest Crisis, Touchline and Childline, but will give legal and general advice. Support is available for the family as a whole, together with money to move house where there is a need, and we will help with arranging holidays, etc.
> In the Childwatch Investigation Unit we deal with offenders, putting together parcels of evidence for the police, and in 1987, 22 paedophiles were prosecuted by the courts.

A Childwatch Information Pack is obtainable from the above address, price 65p.

ISO-SAC In Support of Sexually Abused Children
Angela Rivers
PO Box 526
London NW6 1SU Tel: 01 202-3024

ISO—SAC offers a confidential, non-statutory telephone counselling service for parents of sexually abused children. They are able to answer questions and provide information concerning the involvement of medical, legal and social agencies.

At the 1988 NSPCC Spring Conference, the theory was put forth that sexual abuse is a form of addiction — like alcohol — and should be treated as such. Addicts, being adept at hiding their addiction, make the policy of believing children all-important.

During a workshop on mothers, and another on teenage-girls, it became clear that children often feel that their mothers should (and do) know everything. Angela replies that, in her experience, mothers are, in fact, the last to know.

Kidscape

Michele Elliott
Director
82 Brook Street
London W1Y 1YG
Tel: 01 493-9845

Michele Elliott is director of Kidscape. She is an educational psychologist and has had 17 years' experience working as a counsellor and leader of children's workshops.

Kidscape is the Campaign for Children's Safety. It provides free information for parents about how to keep their children safe from dangers, including the possibility of sexual abuse from anyone — known or unknown. In her book *Keeping Safe* (Hodder and Stoughton, 1988), Michele Elliott writes:

> A young mum contacted Kidscape, suspecting that her six-year-old daughter had been abused. We sent her a free 16-page guide and gave her suggestions on how to talk to with her daughter. The daughter disclosed that the babysitter, an uncle, had been touching her. The mother rang the police and the man was arrested.

Kidscape tries to give guidance to help people make decisions about what to do. If, however, we know that a child is being abused and have the name of the abuser, we will contact the police or social services.

The main aim of Kidscape is to prevent abuse happening and to that end we produce free parents' guides. We also have programmes for schools for children from ages 3 to 18. The programmes include how to deal with bullying, getting lost, and strangers and known adults who might try to harm children.

The founder and director of Kidscape, Michele Elliott, has had several books published in addition to *Keeping Safe*. They include

The Willow Street Kids (Andre Deutsch, 1986).
Nicky and His Friends Stay Safe (Andre Deutsch, 1989).
  Colour picture book for under fives.

For a free copy of the 16-page parents' guide and/or more information about Kidscape, send a large SAE.

Lifeline — family help for violence in the home

Directors: Janine Turner, Pat Hayes
PO Box 251,
Marlborough
Wiltshire SN8 1EA Tel: 0793 731286; 091 413 8566; 0793 47138;
or 0283 226060 Regional numbers are available.

We are a nationwide charity set up in 1984 to help, befriend and support families who are experiencing abuse within the home — physical, mental, emotional and sexual. We are very much a family organization geared to looking at the problems as a whole and not in isolation, working together with outside agencies concerned — probation, marriage guidance, social services, solicitors, family centres, etc.

  Our fundamental belief is in the shared experience — between victims, survivors, survivor and professional, counsellor and professional, abuser and abused. Survivors will get together within their home areas, befriending and supporting one another, linking up with others in the country suffering from like problems, offering them hope. It is important for people who have suffered traumatic and humiliating experiences to be able to externalize their feelings, moving on through a programme of re-education to learn how to cope with the people they are today.

  Victims cannot be helped in isolation when the abuser is still there to destroy further relationships in the future. If an abuser accepts he has a problem and is willing to seek help, then we believe that an abuser can change. To this end, we offer him the same understanding and support as the abused.

  We encourage self-help, believing that it is only by sharing our knowledge and experience and hurt that we can help change the attitudes of the non-believer, take away taboos, and work together towards a better understanding of the problems as a whole.

  Since 1984, when approximately 500 families contacted us for help, our numbers have swelled to around 3,000. Statutory and voluntary agencies refer people to us, and people can contact us direct themselves. We are also a contact service for Childline.

Problems vary from little Jimmy who phones anonymously every time his Mum stands him in a corner with his pants and trousers down, making him feel humiliated and ashamed; to 20-year-old Pete who finds it impossible to make a relationship because of that same kind of abuse he suffered from his mother when he was young. Pete feels all the time that girls are laughing at him, and he feels just as ashamed and abused today as he did all those years ago.

There is Mary who cannot cope with her baby son because of the incest experience she suffered from her stepfather as a child; Bill, who is serving a prison sentence for what he did to his boys; as well as any one of the numerous problems concerned with violence in the home.

Families contact us at the first point at which they feel they have a problem they cannot cope with alone. They can then remain with us for whatever needs they might have. There is no cut-off point. Ongoing support and help by someone they know and trust is invaluable. And as the family moves on, problems encompass a whole range of different issues — domestic violence, sexual abuse, debt, depression, child abuse, difficulties with divorce, and we have a range of leaflets to cover these needs.

We try to provide each family or individual with a friend, some-one who is there for them, for as long as they should need them, and this becomes a vital link after office hours and when many agencies are unavailable over evenings and weekends.

Counselling, ongoing support and advice is offered in a number of ways, depending on whichever feels most comfortable to the person seeking help. Many prefer to correspond, writing out their feelings and posting them out of their lives. Others relate better on the end of a phone, knowing that when they ring, that person is there for them and can relate on a personal level to what it is they feel and need to say. One-to-one counselling can take place within their own home, or at an agency of their choice with which they are in contact, or even in town, depending on what they want to do. The decision and control lies with the person seeking help. It is an essential part of learning to help themselves.

We have nine main telephone numbers as communcation links in Britain, together with numerous other area contacts who will listen, support and advise people within their home area. We have no ongoing funding, and rely totally on donations. Anyone writing should therefore enclose an SAE. Special problem leaflets are charged at 60p, and our quarterly *Friendship* magazine, at £1.00.

MIND — National Association for Mental Health
England: 22 Harley Street
London WlN 2ED Tel: 01 637 0741
Scotland: Angus House
67 York Place
Edinburgh EH3 6AG Tel: 031 556 3062
Ireland: 84 University Street
Belfast BT7 1HE Tel: 0232 28474
Wales: 23 St Mary Street
Cardiff CFl 2AA Tel: 0222 395123

NCH Careline
This is a nationwide telephone counselling service of the National Childrens Home.

Birmingham: 021 440 5970
Luton: 0582 422751
Norwich: 0603 660679
London: 01 514 1177
Leeds: 0532 456456
   Touchline 0532 457777 (9.30 a.m. — 9.30 p.m.)
Maidstone: 0622 56677
Manchester: 061 236 9873
Preston: 0772 24006
Taunton: 0823 333191
Cardiff: 0222 29461
Glasgow: 041 221 6722
Glenrothes: 0592 759651

NCH Careline is a general counselling agency, dealing with all the problems within the community it serves. However with the increased media coverage and growing concern regarding abuse within the home, particularly incest, Carelines throughout the country have seen an increase also in this type of problem.

The majority, although by no means all of our incest clients, come to us as adults. Clients have various reasons for contacting us, but some typical causes are an inability to make lasting relationships; the birth of a baby, or a child reaching the age where incest took place in the mother's childhood; a problem with anorexia, and so on.

Regional Carelines offer various services which can include: telephone counselling, face-to-face counselling, and mobile units which offer advice, counselling and in some cases support to people out in the community. Our telephone counsellors are trained to listen and offer caring support, whatever the person's difficulties. Helping the clients to express their thoughts and feelings is always a part of our counselling. Encouragement and support which help them to face their fears and problems is another aid which it might be necessary to provide. And if the client has begun to feel that he or she is finding counselling beneficial an offer of a face-to-face appointment can be made. Obviously the various regional centres will have slightly different approaches and the following description shows one of the ways that the process could develop.

Once contact has been made, via a unit or by telephone, and an appointment to see a counsellor has been made, the client will receive an initial interview and during this will agree along with the counsellor what the problem is that needs to be worked on and how long this is likely to take. We would normally make a contract of a four- or six-week duration, and renew the contract where necessary. At the start of each and every session the problem to be dealt with is re-evaluated, and at the end of each session a task is set which is designed to help the client begin to solve that particular problem. This method of counselling means that each difficulty the client has is dealt with, and looked at thoroughly and equally by both parties. In this way, each door which is reached is opened, gone through, and closed behind us as we move through the problem areas.

One client came to us on the anniversary of the death of her father. She had been abused by him in every way, including sexually, and had little or no memory of her childhood years from the time of the sexual abuse. She had lived with a man who, turn, both physically and sexually abused her. He left her when she became pregnant, and the baby, which she adored, died whilst still very young. She had several casual relationships and one more serious one, which was getting nowhere and causing her some unhappiness. Her family, when finally told about the incest, refused to believe it had taken place, although the client knew that at least three other members of the family witnessed it take place on one occasion. The client had also been abducted by some youths, who repeatedly raped her. She suffered at the hands of the police when this was reported, and her family were embarrassed by what had happened and offered little or no support.

Clearly, this client had many and varied problems on which to work. She felt worthless and disliked herself for the shame she had brought on her family. She had to learn that almost everything that had happened to her had been done to her and not caused by her. In areas where she had failed to be a 'good' person, she needed to understand why. She had to learn to apportion blame where necessary and then to forgive those people she blamed. She had to build on her strength so that she could stand apart from her family if they would not accept her, without feeling that they had rejected her for her 'badness'. She went with her counsellor to visit her father's grave and told him what she felt about him. Even in death, he terrified her. She spent several sessions looking at the negative areas of her life, guilt, blame, and so on, and several more where she could see hope and a way through.

Each subject was dealt with in the way she wanted it to be and she agreed with the counsellor which things were of real relevance, so the objectives were clear to them both at all times. She received counselling for nine months and was, in her own opinion, a completely different woman at the end of it. On the whole, she had done everything in her own way and time, with the counsellor there to help her. She wound down her visits at the end until she reached a point where she herself broke off contact with the agency.

At Careline all cases are dealt with in strict confidence, regardless of the age of the client or the nature of the problem. We work with the family, the individual, the victim or the perpetrator, as necessary.

The whole basis of our counselling is to enable our clients to

182 Home is where the hurt is

improve their lives in the way they want, to help them discover where necessary what that way is, and to work with them in a positive way to help them begin to live a happy life.

Incest and child abuse are subjects which people find shocking and difficult to understand. Such behaviour, which can do untold damage to all involved, cannot be condoned. But, from the experiences of those like the client in the case study, an optimistic message is sounded, a ray of hope is seen and, at the same time, a challenge is presented to society. Without the support of a listening, caring and committed friend (as in the form of a counsellor) individuals who suffer from the trauma of abuse, whatever its form, have little means left at their disposal to rebuild their lives. Perhaps we have experienced trauma, anxiety and debilitating fears and been abused by insults, aggression, inconsideration and a host of other things which harm our relationships with others. In seeking help to cope with the situation, we were looking for someone who would understand and be with us in the experience which was causing us difficulty.

From our own awareness then, we can recognise the challenge presented to us by the experience of victims of sexual, physical, moral or other forms of abuse. Child abuse, which all of us find difficult to face, needs in all its aspects our attention, caring and understanding. Those who have suffered, or are suffering, need the more noble qualities that do exist in society if they are to be happy with themselves and life once more.

NCH Careline

NSPCC — The National Society for the Prevention of Cruelty to Children
67 Saffron Hill
London EC1N 8RS Tel: 01 242 1626

The NSPCC has a network of teams in operation, known as Child Prevention Teams (CPTs). The telephone number for your local CPT can be found in Yellow Pages, or through British Telecom Directory Enquiries. If you live in the London area you could call your local CPT, or the NSPCC Child Protection Line London on 01 404 4447

While different CPTs offer different services, all teams offer:

- A 24-hour telephone service to give advice and to take referrals from members of the public or professionals

- An investigation, treatment and assessment service.

The NSPCC works closely with other local professionals, including local authority social workers, health visitors, family doctors, and the police. If your local team feels you would receive more appropriate help from another agency, they will ensure that you are put in touch with the right people.

All teams work on the basis that:

- Children are the first object of concern

- If a child, or someone else, claims that they have been abused in any way, they will always be believed unless or until there is strong evidence that this is not the case

- Parents, or other family members, will be involved wherever possible. The NSPCC aims to work with parents, not to undermine them. However, in some cases, a child may be taken to a safe place in order to protect them.

If any individual is concerned about a child, or feels that their own previous experiences as a child are affecting their family life, they should seek help. All NSPCC staff are qualified and trained. They will not be shocked by anything you tell them, and they will not seek to make moral judgements. Teams deal with calls from many women and men.

The first step is usually a telephone call from an individual or organization referred to the local CPT by another agency, such as a social services department. In emergency cases, the team will respond quickly with a visit to the home, or by ensuring that another professional visits.

Once contact has been made, there will be a thorough investigation of the case and an assessment will be made. This will be carried out sympathetically and sensitively. Traumatic events in childhood cause immense pain and anguish; reviving or explaining these events can be equally painful. CPT staff are trained to help individuals in such a way that the process of assessment or treatment does not add to the initial trauma.

Treatment plans are tailored to individual needs. Treatment

might, for example, involve attending an NSPCC Family Centre, individual counselling and therapy, or working with a group of people who have similar experiences. Children and adults are encouraged to express the anger and pain they may be feeling.

Child sexual abuse is often called the 'best kept secret'. Any child or adult who has been sexually abused should seek help. People who have been abused are not 'guilty'; responsibility lies with the abuser, not the abused.

The effects of abuse may be passed on to the next generation. A mother who has been abused may, for example, experience great anxiety about her own children, or feel unable to form a stable relationship with the child's father.

Modern family life can be very complicated and confusing. If you have been sexually abused, or feel that you need to discuss a family problem, please contact the NSPCC, or one of the other agencies mentioned in this book. Caring help and counselling helps both children and adults, and can ensure that the effects of abuse are not passed on to other children.

Parentline — OPUS (Organization for Parents Under Stress)
106 Godstone Road
Whyteleafe CR3 0EB Tel: 01 645 0505

The telephone number given above is a 24-hour recorded message, and gives the number of the group on call. For details of groups operating nationwide contact: 01 645 0469.

Parentline Groups aim to break the cycle of family unhappiness and child abuse by enabling parents to share the difficulties of bringing up children with other parents.

Parentline volunteers offer telephone helpline and befriending services to all parents, both those who are in crisis and those who simply feel they need to talk about the problems. Isolation and stress are among the major factors leading to abuse of all kinds.

Parentline groups operate at varying times, are all run by volunteers who are parents themselves, and the services are very cost effective.

Parentline volunteers offer a confidential and anonymous service to other parents. This has proved to be a stepping stone in situations where a child is at risk — the first step to obtaining the professional help needed. At other times it has acted as a safety valve, taking the pressure out of parent and child conflict.

Rape crisis centre
PO Box 69
London WC1X 9NJ

Area rape crisis telephone numbers can be found in directories, or by asking at your local Citizen's Advice Bureau.

RSSPCC — Royal Scottish Society for the Prevention of Cruelty to Children
Melville House
41 Polwarth Terrace
Edinburgh EH11 1NU Tel: 031 3378539

If you live in Scotland, you can either phone or write to the address above for help, or look in your local telephone directory for your area number.

Samaritans
You can ring any Samaritan Centre at any time and visit almost all without appointment any day or evening of the week: you can also write.

Local Samaritan Centres are listed in the phone book.

Social Services
The telephone number and address of your local Social Services office will be listed in your area telephone numbers if you need to contact them after office hours.

Regional centres

Avon Sexual Abuse Centre
Tel: Bristol 0272 428331

Bedfordshire Sexual Abuse Help Line (incorporating Luton Rape Crisis Centre)
Tel: 0582 33592

We are a counselling and support service, open from Monday to

Friday 9 a.m. — 5 p.m., and Saturdays from 10 a.m. — 12 p.m.

We offer telephone and one-to-one counselling and we have one group at present, led by a counsellor, for women who have been sexually abused as children. We have also a self-help group for women who have been raped as adults.

Bristol Crisis Service for Women
c/o The Women's Centre
44 The Grove
Bristol BS1 Tel: 0272 354105

There is a growing amount of energy and commitment being directed towards the need of women who are in some kind of emotional distress.

In 1984, an umbrella organization called the 'Women and Mental Health Network' was formed in Bristol and was made up of women who had some contact and interest in the mental health system.

The network met regularly to look at the needs of women going through periods of deep emotional distress and unhappiness which made them feel isolated and vulnerable.

Although the network itself eventually disbanded, a couple of projects arose which are now flourishing and causing some interest around the country — the Bristol Crisis Service for Women, and Womankind (for Womankind see end of Directory, under its own heading).

The Bristol Crisis Service for Women is a new project which arose in April 1986. Since that time we have been looking at the needs of women in crisis, especially those who injure themselves as a way of expressing their distress.

In response to our research into the needs of women in distress, we have found that there is a special need for some kind of support which operates outside of normal working hours when other services have closed.

Initially, we have begun by providing a telephone helpline which is open on Friday and Saturday evenings from 9 p.m. to 12.30 a.m.

Our service, which opened on 22 January 1988, is a specialized women-only concern. We feel that giving our callers the reassurance of knowing that they will be listened to and supported by another woman will inspire feelings of safety and confidence.

The women who answer the phones are all volunteers trained

in telephone counselling. Many of us have been through periods of crisis in our own lives; some have experienced self harm; some are survivors of the mental health system. We feel these experiences are important in helping us listen to a woman in crisis with understanding and respect.

Any woman who rings will be listened to and will be offered counselling which is non-judgemental and accepting. Sometimes, for a woman who feels very much isolated with her distress, this may be the first chance she has had to talk about her feelings. We believe the experience of being listened to for as long as it takes is an important first step towards working through feelings which may seem overwhelming.

We maintain a directory of local and national groups so that we can refer women on, when appropriate, if they have specific problems such as addiction, sexual abuse, tranquillizer withdrawal, etc.

Working alongside the two projects mentioned above — the Bristol Crisis Service for Women, and Womankind (see Womankind under its own heading at end of directory) — is an organization called Missing Link, for single homeless women in need of some support. Currently, it has four houses providing 15 bed spaces. Each resident receives support from her 'Key Worker' on a regular basis (at the moment there are four workers) and women can stay for a period of up to four years.

For all these projects as well as other mental health organizations, there is an increasing need for a more intensive kind of support for women who might otherwise end up in hospital. When feeling desperate, vulnerable and unable to cope with their lives, many women look to (or are taken into) psychiatric hospital. For most, psychiatric care cannot cover their deep emotional needs and this can heighten feelings of powerlessness and isolation. Taking charge over one's own life then becomes almost impossible. Currently, there is no alternative to hospitalization.

With this in mind, we are trying to reconvene the Bristol Women and Mental Health Network, but to include as many women as possible who have an interest in mental health. We hope to gain and share knowledge and experience with the ultimate aim of opening a sanctuary or refuge. This would be for women whose need to feel safe and supported whilst working through an emotional crisis far outweighs anything the psychiatrist can offer.

Cumbria Rape Crisis Centre

Tel: 0539 25255. Monday 7 p.m. — 10 p.m. and Wednesday 12 p.m. — 3 p.m.

Incest Helpline (Wales)

PO Box 350
Cardiff CF1 3XR Tel: 0222 733929

We are a Cardiff-based confidential telephone counselling service for incest survivors. We can offer a confidential telephone counselling service to any person who has suffered sexual abuse. It does not matter how, by whom or how long ago it happened. We can also offer help to parents whose children have been or are being abused.

Firstly, we offer sympathetic and confidential telephone counselling to help people express their feelings about their experiences and to reassure them that the responsibility for what has happened lies completely with the abuser.

Secondly, we encourage people to join self-help groups to meet others who have had similar experiences and to help one another rebuild their confidence.

Thirdly, we act as a referral point for individual counselling.

Incest Helpline members are also involved in educational and campaign work with the general public and with relevant agencies such as social services, medical staff, schools and voluntary agencies. We are also keen to help other similar groups set up so that, in time, a network of such groups will exist throughout Wales.

The Helpline is available between 6.30 p.m. and 10.30 p.m. most evenings. At other times you may get an answerphone to leave a message, or you can write if you wish.

London Rape Crisis Centre

PO Box 69
London WC1X 9NJ Tel: 01 837 1600

Oasis Centre (London)

Directors: Penny and Ray Edwards
Tel: 01 340 3924

The Oasis Centre is a private counselling and psychotherapy centre staffed by a husband and wife team, funded entirely by the fees paid by the clients. Each consultation is confidential and the centre has no links with any statutory body.

Ray Edwards is a Gestalt therapist with healing and hypnotherapy experience. One of his interests is in helping people to come to terms with their sexual orientation and he occasionally works as co-therapist with his wife Penny when engaged in couple or family therapy.

Penny Edwards is a counsellor using client centred approaches taken from Gestalt psychology, TA, body work, etc., as appropriate. She is a trained masseuse and applied kinesiologist who also uses acupressure to relieve physical and/or emotional pain. Her interest lies in the effect of food stuffs on emotional states, and the clients' relationship with what they eat is a prime area for 'work'. She uses a non-evasive way of testing for food sensitivity and will give nutritional guidance as appropriate.

All clients are seen by appointment only. Penny works in Basildon (Essex) and the City Health Centre as well as in East Finchley.

Sanctuary
Rosina Godfrey and Chris Underwood
PO Box 23
Gillingham
Kent
Telephone: 0634 378300

Sanctuary offers a free impartial confidential telephone counselling service from Monday to Saturday 4.00 p.m. — 10.00 p.m. It also incorporates on the same number the Birds n' Beeline for the under-18-year-olds with emotional or sexual worries.

After one year, Sanctuary is operating from its own premises in High Street, Rainham, Kent.

During 1986 and 1987, they received applications from 77 people who wanted to work on the line at Sanctuary. Eleven were finally taken on and were trained to man the phone. During 1987, they helped over 200 families to cope with the trauma of sexual abuse. Callers' ages range from 10 to 84 and they ring on all kinds of subjects: past and present abuse, rape and incest, how to talk to a young girl who is behaving out of character, and so on.

They have provided speakers for various groups of people, a home for disturbed girls, Church groups, and other community based groups.

They have formed Friends of Sanctuary to take over the fund-raising activities, leaving the Sanctuary organizers to concentrate on the helpline and its volunteers.

Expansion in the future will take the form of extending the hours and offering face-to-face counselling of parents. As one mother said: 'My daughter is taken care of, he's been put away, but no-one thinks of poor old Mum!' Well, now someone does have time for her. Over half the calls are from Mums (and Dads) who are faced with the task of caring for their child in very difficult circumstances.

A long-term view is to provide a safe house or hostel for the over-16s who have suffered abuse and need somewhere safe to stay, so that they can talk over the situation and discuss what steps may be taken to remedy the situation.

The Edinburgh Association for Mental Health
EAMH
40 Shandwick Place
Edinburgh EH2 4RT
Tel: 031 225 8508

EAMH is an independent voluntary organization. We have a number of objectives relating to mental health with special emphasis on the needs of those living in or returning to the community and experiencing mental illness or other mental health problems.

Our team of EAMH staff and volunteers are trained and experienced counsellors. We offer an opportunity to talk freely and confidentially about matters of concern to you in the area of mental health. For example, we may be able to help with personal problems, personal or family relationships or concern for family members or friends who may have mental health problems. We can also provide information about other agencies if required.

Anyone can use the service, and you can come on your own or with someone else. Sessions last for up to one hour. You can come and see us just once or we can offer longer term counselling.

We prefer you to make an appointment either by phoning or coming in, but you can drop in during daytime counselling hours and you will be seen if a counsellor is free:

Tuesdays: 5.15 p.m. to 7.15 p.m.
Thursdays: 2.00 p.m. to 4.00 p.m.

The Women's Therapy Centre (London)
6 Manor Gardens
London N7 6LA Tel: 01 263 6200

The Centre provides long- and short-term therapy for women, both one-to-one and in groups. We also offer a programme of workshops every term on topics of special interest to women.

Womankind (Bristol)
Pamela Trevithick
Bristol Settlement
43 Ducie Road
Bristol BS5 0AX

Womankind grew out of the Bristol Women and Mental Health Network which was started in June 1984 as an umbrella organization made up of women who had had some contact with the mental health system as patients or ex-patients (survivors), relatives, friends, workers, activists, lovers. Not long after we began to meet, it became clear that there was a need for a project where women could go for help.

Womankind began in 1986, and today we run two weekly drop-in groups, one for women who are experiencing some kind of depression and one for women coming off tranquillizers. We encourage women to telephone one another or to meet up whenever they can. This is important because most women who come into contact with Womankind express intense feelings of loneliness and isolation as well as a great deal of confusion about the different messages or advice they've been given, the most painful and confusing being 'pull yourself together'.

On a day-to-day basis, we try to keep our office and telephone link open as much as possible, so that we can listen to women in distress, answer queries, put women in touch with other organizations and provide information about Womankind and what groups we run. To do this we rely heavily on the commitment of a number of unpaid workers (volunteers) most of whom, like the paid workers, have had some kind of psychiatric treatment and have suffered different degrees of discrimination because of their psychiatric history, particularly in employment. Some unpaid workers see their involvement with Womankind as a first step to getting a job, whilst others use the contact to unravel what's been happening to them and to discover what they want to do next. For women who want to learn new skills, we run courses on counselling, word processing, etc., and we also have a small budget to pay for outside courses (such as assertiveness training).

We see the over-representation of women in mental health statistics as a direct consequence of the inequality and discrimination that women experience in society, which can be seen in the lack of status or recognition given to women. For example, it is estimated that over twice as many women as men are likely to be diagnosed as depressed and the rates are higher for working class women. In the case of agoraphobia, between 75 and 88 per cent of all those diagnosed are said to be women and a similar picture occurs in a anorexia nervosa where it's estimated that 90 per cent of those diagnosed are women. Women have more hospital admissions for psychiatric disorders, consult their GPs more, are given more psychotropic (mood altering) drugs, like Valium and Ativan, have more repeat prescriptions, and women's dependency on alcohol is growing at an alarming rate. For us, this makes mental health very much a women's issue.

In Bristol, we are fortunate to have other mental health projects for women running alongside us. These include Missing Link, a housing project for single homeless women, and a Women's Crisis Service, a telephone helpline for women at weekends. In addition, we're in regular contact with other voluntary groups for women and men like Windmill Hill City Farm, the newly formed Bristol Patients Forum (Survivors Speak Out), Bristol MIND and Friend at Weston-Super-Mare.

Yet, despite our success in starting projects, we have also borne much grief and disappointment, particularly in relation to women who felt unable to keep going or to fight back. Early last year, we were shattered by the suicide of Jane Hartley, who was involved in most of the projects mentioned above. Jane's courage and commitment to women will long be remembered and her tragic death is a painful reminder that when we're fighting to change the mental health system, we're fighting for women's lives.

Pamela Trevithick
Development Worker
Womankind

Directory of advisory services in the USA and Canada

There are numerous prevention and treatment programs throughout the United States both for victims, survivors and the offenders, and to really find out about and understand what each one is about it is essential to go to source, to question, to collect relevant information, to speak out about experiences, and to find the right one for you.

● **CAPP** — The Child Assault Prevention Project — is a means of teaching children how to remain safe, strong and free through role-playing the kind of situations they might meet in everyday life. Children are encouraged to use their own resources to solve problems, and this is important because in unsafe situations it is often the adults they would normally ask who are the danger.

● **CSATP** — Child Sexual Abuse Treatment Program — was begun in 1971, since which time the Santa Clara group has become the largest in the country, coping with over 600 families a year. It is also the National group for Parents United, Daughters and Sons United, and Women Molested as Children United.

Additional information can be obtained by contacting:

The National Center for Child Abuse and Neglect Clearing House,
PO Box 1182,
Washington, DC 20013.

In areas of America where there are no programs, it is essential that victims do not give up and accept what they have as a way of life. You don't have to suffer. People are there to help. But you have to be prepared to work at helping yourself in order to find what best works for you. Try contacting your local Women's Center, Women-Against-Rape groups, parent centers and health-care groups. Learn to speak out about your experience. You have nothing about which to feel ashamed.

National networks

National runaway switchboard
(One out of every three runaways are thought to be escaping sexual abuse.)

Dial toll-free: 1-800-621-4000. (In Illinois, it is 1-800-972-6004.)

A staff of trained volunteers and professionals can answer questions about incest and sexual abuse. They can also put callers in contact with appropriate organizations within their home area, connecting callers direct with an agency while they stay on the line.

Parents United/Daughters and Sons United
PO Box 952, San José, California 95104. Phone: 1-408-280-5055.

Information on self-help support groups for offenders and victims.

National Center for the Prevention and Treatment of Child Abuse
University of Colorado Medical Center, 1001 Jasmine Street, Denver, Colorado 80220

This is an organization providing treatment, research and training for abusive families and abused children.

Parents Anonymous
22330 Hawthorn Blvd. Suite 208, Torrance, California 90505. (213) 371-3501.

A national self-help organization for parents using group therapy and positive parenting methods to help abusing parents change their behaviour. There are many local groups in communities throughout the United States.

Regional organizations

ALASKA
The Judith Group
Box 2334
Soldatna, AK 99669

CALIFORNIA

Parents United
Child Sexual Abuse Treatment
  Program
PO Box 952
San José, CA 95108

ARIZONA
Center Against Sexual Assault
137 West McDowell Road
Phoenix, AZ 85003

Sacremento Rape Crisis Center
2224 J Street
Sacramento, CA 95816

CALIFORNIA *continued*

Child Sexual Abuse Treatment
  Program
Dept of Public Welfare
Dependent Children Section
6950 Levant Street
San Diego, CA 92111

Child Assault Prevention Project
(CAPP)
Berkeley Children's Services
1017 University Avenue
Berkeley, CA 94710

COLORADO

Child Sexual Abuse Treatment
  Program
University of Colorado Medical
  Center
4200 East 9th Avenue
Denver, CO 80262

Child Protective Services
El Paso County Department of
  Social Services
PO Box 2692
105 N. Spruce
Colorado Springs, CO 80901

DISTRICT OF COLUMBIA

Child Sexual Victim Assistance
  Project
Child Protection Center
Children's Hospital National
Medical Center
111 Michigan Avenue
Washington, DC 20010

FLORIDA

Child Sexual Abuse Treatment
  Program
Tampa Women's Health Center,
Inc
3004 Fletcher
Tampa, FL 33612

GEORGIA

Rape Crisis Center
Grady Memorial Hospital
80 Butler Street, S.E.
Atlanta, GA 30303

HAWAII

Sexual Abuse Treatment Center
Kapiolani Children's Hospital
1319 Punahoo Street
Honolulu, HI 96826

ILLINOIS

Childhood Sexual Abuse Project
(CAUSES)
836 West Wellington Avenue
Chicago, Il. 60657

Child Sexual Abuse Treatment
  Program
Community Service Council of
  Northern Illinois
757 Luther Drive
Romeoville, Il. 60441

KANSAS

Wyandotte County Mental
  Health Center
Eaton at 36th Street
Kansas City, KS 66103

Child Sexual Abuse Treatment
  Program
Child Protective Services
Department of Social and
  Rehabilitation Services
1 Patrons Plaza
Olathe, KS 66061

MAINE

Project Response
232 Main Street
Waterville, ME 04330

MARYLAND

*Sexual Abuse Treatment
Program*
Baltimore City Department of
Social Services
312 East Oliver Street
Baltimore, MD 21202

Child Sexual Abuse Program
Protective Services Unit
Montgomery Co. Dept of Social
Services
5630 Fishers Lane
Rockville, MD 20852

MINNESOTA

*Child Sexual Abuse Treatment
Program*
East Side Neighbourhood
Service, Inc.
1929 Second Street, N.E.
Minneapolis, MN 55418

NEW JERSEY

*Atlantic County Adolescent
Maltreatment Project*
Division of Youth and Family
Services
26 S Pennsylvania Avenue
Atlantic City, NJ 08401

Incest Counselling Program
Mercer County Division of
Youth and Family Services
1901 North Olden Avenue
Trenton, NJ 08618

MASSACHUSETTS

Sexual Abuse Treatment Team
Children's Hospital Medical
Center
300 Longwood Avenue
Boston, MA 02115

Protective Services Unit
Massachusetts Department of
Public Welfare
75 Commercial Street
Brockton, MA 02402

MICHIGAN

*Child Sexual Abuse Treatment
Program*
Children's Aid Society
71 West Warren Street
Detroit, MI 48201

MISSOURI

*Child Sexual Abuse Management
Program*
St Louis Children's Hospital
500 South Kingshighway Blvd
PO Box 14871
St Louis, MO 63178

NEW MEXICO

*Sexual Abuse Demonstration
Project*
New Mexico Dept. of Human
Services
Family Resource Centre —
Team 3
919 Vassar N.E.
Albuquerque, NM 87106

NEW YORK

*New York Society for the
  Prevention of Cruelty to
  Children*
110 East 71st Street
New York, NY 10021

NORTH DAKOTA

Rape Crisis Center
Grand Folks Co. Social
  Services Center
118 North 3rd Street
Grand Forks, ND 58201

*The Rape and Crisis Abuse
  Center*
PO Box 1655
Fargo, ND S8107

OKLAHOMA

Children's Protection Unit
444 S Houston
Tulsa, OK 74105

PENNSYLVANIA

*Incest Counselling Program and
  Innonsense*
(Rape Group for Women
  Victims
Women Organized Against Rape
  in Bucks Co.
PO Box 793
Langhorne, PA 19047

The Joseph J Peters Institute
formerly the Center for Rape
  Concern)
12 South 16th Street, 11th Floor
Philadelphia, PA 19102

NORTH CAROLINA

*North Carolina Sexual Abuse
  Identification and Treatment
  Project*
Department of Human Resources
Department of Social Services
325 N. Salisbury Street
Raleigh, NC 27611

OHIO

*Sexual Abuse Treatment/Training
  Project*
Federation for Community
  Planning
1001 Huron Road
Cleveland, OH 44115

*Child Assault Prevention
  Program*
Women Against Rape
PO Box 02084
Columbus, OH 43202

OREGAN

Child Protective Services
1031 E. Burnside
Portland, OR 97215

TEXAS

Dallas Sexual Abuse Project
Texas Dept of Human Resources
Social Services Branch
John H Reagan Building
Austin, TX 78701

Sexual Abuse Unit
Dallas County MHMR Center
5925 Maple Avenue, Suite 113
Dallas, TX 75235

TENNESSEE

PAASAC
(Project Against Appalachian
  Sex Abuse of Children)
Child and Family Services of
  Knox County
114 Dameron Avenue
Knoxville, TN 37219

VIRGINIA

*Virginia Dept of Social
  Services*
Municipal Center
Virginia Beach, VA 23456

WASHINGTON

Sexual Assault Center
Harborview Medical Center
325 9th Avenue
Seattle, WA 98104

*Juvenile Sex Offender Treatment
  Program*
Adolescent Clinic
Child Development and Mental
  Retardation Department
University of Washington
Seattle, WA 98195

*Child Sexual Abuse Treatment
  Program*
Child Protective Services
1310 Tacoma Avenue
Tacoma, WA 98404

UTAH

Rape Crisis Center
Core 10 Program
329 East 6th South
Salt Lake City, UT 84111

WEST VIRGINIA

*Sexual Abuse Treatment and
  Training*
3375 Route 60 East
PO Box 8069
Huntingdon, WV 25705

WISCONSIN

Parental Stress Center
1506 Madison Street
Madison, WI 53711

Sexual Assault Treatment Center
Social Services Department
Family Hospital
2711 West Wells Street
Milwaukee, WI 53208

Canada

In Canada on January 4th 1983, a new criminal law about assault and
sexual offences came into force. It abolished the old offences of 'rape',
'attempted rape', 'indecent rape', 'indecent assault female' and 'indecent
assault male'. In their place, the new law made sexual offences a form
of assault. While not defining exactly what the term 'sexual assault' might
mean, it has come to be any form of sexual activity — kissing, fondling

or sexual intercourse with another without his or her consent. And the judge and jury are left to decide in any particular case whether or not there was a sexual assault.

The new law means victims of sexual offences have new protection in court. In court, the law restricts the types of questions the victim can be asked, and the rules of proof now apply to sexual offences as to other crimes.

For the offender, the minimum penalty in the first case is six months in jail. And because the procedure and penalty now depend on how severe was the sexual assault, the penalty could be up to ten years in jail.

If you are a victim, a survivor or an offender living in Canada, look at the kind of person you are and get help. Don't accept pain and abuse as a way of life.

If it isn't immediately obvious where you can go, then contact one of the agencies below and ask about help within your home area.

Canadian Society for the Prevention of Cruelty to Children (CSPCC)
PO Box 700, Midland, Ontario L4R 4P4.

King County Rape Relief
305 So. 43rd. Renton, WA 98055, Canada.

Advisory Services in Australia and New Zealand

Australia

Women for Survival
PO Box 53
North Fremantle
Western Australia, 6160

Incest Survivors Association
PO Box 8311
Stirling Street
Perth
Western Australia, 6000

New Zealand

Contacts are available for families needing help at the back of every telephone book in the Yellow Pages headed Community Welfare Organizations.

Bibliography

The books listed are for and about people with child sexual abuse as a part of their life experience.

Books for children on resisting sexual abuse

Caren Adams *No is not Enough: Helping teenagers avoid sexual assault* (Impact Publishers, USA, 1984).
A parents' guide. Also good for teenagers themselves to read.

Ellen Adams and Marti Betz *I like you to make jokes with me, but I don't want you to touch me* (Lollipop Power, Inc., USA. 1981).

Michele Elliott *Keeping Safe* (Hodder and Stoughton, 1988).
A parents' step-by-step guide to talking with children about keeping safe.

Jennifer Fay and B Flerchinger *Top Secret: Sexual assault information for teenagers only* (King County Rape Relief, USA, 1982).
An attractive book in pop format with graphics, imparting good information and advice.

Lory Freeman *Its my body: A book to teach young children how to resist uncomfortable touch* (Parenting Press, Inc., USA, 1982).
A lovely book, with pictures, for reading aloud to pre-school children, age two to five, with phrases such as: 'Don't do that!' for them to practice saying 'as if they really mean it'.

Sherryll Kerns Kraizer *The Safe Child: The commonsense approach to protecting your children* (Futura, 1985).
A parents' guide about dealing with prevention of abduction and sexual abuse of children between the ages of three and twelve; covering subjects such as strangers, relatives, friends, teachers, day nurseries and the latch-key life.

Robin Lennit with Bob Crane *It's Okay to say no!* (Thorsons, 1986) shows how children can protect themselves against sexual abuse by people they know as well as strangers.

Frank Smith *It's OK to say no! activity book* (Peter Haddock, 1985).
Games, puzzles, pictures to colour in, mazes — all dealing with sexual assault of children.

Frank Smith *It's OK to say no! colouring book* (Peter Haddock, 1985).
Pictures to colour in for four-year-olds and upwards, with explanatory text adults can read aloud.

Oralee Wachter *No more secrets for me* (Viking, 1985).
Four good stories with black and white pictures by Caroline Binch. For children aged 7-11. Stories illustrate what a child's rights are, what situations might be risky, how to prevent sexual abuse, and what to do if you are abused. The first British book.

Books published abroad are available from:
Sisterwrite Bookshop
190 Upper Street
London N1 1RQ
Tel: 01 226 9782

Silver Moon Bookshop
68 Charing Cross Road
London WC2
Tel: 01 836 7906

For further information and advice about the books write to:
ISICSA
24 Blackheath Rise
London SE13 7PN Tel: 01 852 7432

Books young people might like to read

Maya Angelou *I know why the caged bird sings* (Virago, 1983).
An autobiography.

Ellen Bass and Louise Thornton *I never told anyone: Writings by women survivors of child sexual abuse* (Harper & Row, 1983).
Women tell their own stories.

Katherine Brady *Father's Day: A true story of incest* (Dell Books, 1979).
'. . .the two things I needed most, but had to wait years to hear: you are not alone and you are not to blame.'

Nawal El Saadawi *Woman at point zero* (Zed Books, 1983).
A novel. 'I am saying that you are all criminals, all of you: the fathers, the uncles, the husbands, the pimps, the lawyers, the doctors, the journalists, and all men of all professions.'

Kitty Fitzgerald *Marje* (Sheba Feminist Publishers, 1984).
A novel. 'Understanding lets the evil grow. Anger will stop it.'

Toni McNaron and Yarrow Morgan *Voices in the night* (Cleis Press, USA, 1982).
First-person accounts.

Lynda Morgan *Megan's secrets* (Papers, Inc., New Zealand, 1987).
A novel. 'Telling is what makes us free, telling it like it was, the way it really happened, the truth.'

Sarah Nelson *Incest: Fact and Myth* (Stremullion, 1987).
A concise and radical study of incest.

Richard Peck, *Are you in the house alone?* (Pan, 1976).
A novel about rape of a 16-year-old by her best friend's boyfriend.

Margaret Randall *This is about incest* (Firebrand books, USA, 1987).
A survivor works through her childhood experiences of sexual abuse by her grandfather. Prose, family photographs and poems.

Joan Riley *The unbelonging* (Women's Press, 1985). A novel about a Jamaican girl who comes to England when she is 11.

Miriam Saphira *The sexual abuse of children* (Papers Inc. New Zealand, 1985).
'This book has been written to give information on the sexual abuse of children to parents, counsellors, government departments, and the girls themselves.'

Flora Rheta Schreiber *Sybil* (Penguin, 1973).
The true story of a woman with sixteen personalities — two of whom were men — and her struggle, against overwhelming odds, for health and happiness.

Jacqueline Spring *Cry Hard and Swim: The story of an incest survivor* (Virago, 1987).
An autobiography. '. . .there came to us survivors the realisation that we are not different, that we are neither victims nor heroines. . .'

Alice Walker *The Color Purple* (Women's Press, 1983).
A beautifully written novel, full of wisdom.

Books published abroad are available from Sisterwrite Bookshop and from Silver Moon Bookshop, whose addresses are on p. 202.

Important articles on incest and child sexual abuse

Anonymous, 'Breaking the silence', *Social Work Today,* 17 November 1986.
A survivor's account of sadistic abuse by grandfather from age 2 to 15.
'Grandfather took me into the church cellar . . . He showed me the church boiler and opened its door revealing a fiery hell . . . I was told that if I didn't obey I'd be thrown on this fire . . .'

Annette Bradbury, 'A model of treatment', in *Community Care:* 4, September 1986.
A case history describing treatment, and similarity to bereavement. 'They do not forgive their father, and given the nature of the abuse, I doubt if they will ever truly forgive him.'

Patricia Cummings and Gabrielle Hall, 'Report on planning and running a girls' group', 1987
History and development of SAIF-Line group, selection of girls, planning and preparing 10 sessions, evaluation. Available from SAIF-Line
The Link Centre
7 Southbrook Terrace
Bradford 7

David Gough, 'The child witness: Do the courts abuse children?' in *Child Abuse Review,* 1:5, Spring 1987.
The believability of children and how to achieve a more realistic assessment of the evidence children provide.
Charlotte Mitra, 'Judicial discourse in father-daughter incest appeal cases', in *International Journal of Sociology of Law,* 12, 1987.
'. . . the decisions made by the Court of Appeal in incest cases support the dominant ideology of patriarchal power.'

Anne Peake, 'Outline for monitoring young children' *in Ed. psychologist schools*

Counselling of children

Outline for monitoring children in secondary schools

Planning and organising group work for older children

Discussion paper re: child sexual abuse prevention programs in schools
From CSACS
Keston Centre
Keston Road
London N17 6PW

Simone Reed 'A voluntary worker's view of the professionals'. Talk given to British Psychological Society, 1987. £250 from Simone Reed (founder of Crisis Line).
39 Riverbank
Lower Beach Road
Shoreham-by-Sea
Sussex BN4 5YH

Jacqui Roberts, 'Fostering the sexually abused child', in *Adoption and Fostering,* 10: 1, 1986.
Includes the problems a sexually abused child brings to the foster home, behaviour problems in younger children and in older children.

Gerrilyn Smith, 'Child sexual abuse: The power of intrusion', *Adoption and Fostering,* 10: 3, 1986
For those working with girls, or with foster parents.

Eternal vigilance: The price of safety. Recognition of child sexual abuse and strategies for change.

In care: The sexually abused child What is child sexual abuse? Signs and symptoms; how it happens; what it involves.
Right solution incorrectly applied. Verbal and non-verbal behaviour of sexually abused children; the double bind
From CSACS
Keston Centre
Keston Road
London N17 6PW

Terry, 'How I survived sexual abuse', in *Foster Care,* June 1986.
'. . . I started to look on Austin as my sexual mentor. After all, I trusted him and he wouldn't do anything to harm me, would he?'

Richard White, 'Videotaping children's disclosure of sexual abuse', *Child Abuse Review,* 1: 5, Spring 1987.
How to interview a child so that evidence is acceptable in law.
N. J. Wild and J. M. Wynne, 'Child sex rings', in *British Medical Journal,* 293: 19, 1986.
Study of 11 child sex rings in Leeds — 14 adult male perpetrators and 175 children aged 6 to 15.

Dr Wilkins, 'Family nudity and incest', in *Child Abuse Review*, 1: 5, 1987.
The opportunities for abuse in seemingly harmless practices.

Dr Wilson, 'Child sexual abuse histories among professionals', in *Child Abuse Review*, 1: 7, 1987.
Surveys of professionals in Canada and Britain. Approximately half of women professionals had experienced sexual abuse as children; and about a quarter of male professionals.

Dr Jane Wynne 'Child sexual abuse: Medical examination', in *Child Abuse Review*, 1: 5, 1987.
Details of how the examination is conducted, (internal examination *not* performed routinely) and diagnosis.

The above named articles are all in British journals. Where shown, they are available direct from their authors.

Index